SEEN AND HEARD

TEENAGERS TALK ABOUT THEIR LIVES

SEEN AND HEARD

AUG 3 2004

Published in 1998 and distributed in the U.S. by
STEWART, TABORI & CHANG,
a division of U.S. Media Holdings, Inc.
115 West 18th Street, New York, NY 10011

Distributed in Canada by
GENERAL PUBLISHING COMPANY LTD.
30 Lesmill Road
Don Mills, Ontario, Canada M3B 2T6

Sold in Australia by
PERIBO PTY LTD.
58 Beaumont Road
Mount Kuring-gai, NSW 2080, Australia

Distributed in all other territories by
GRANTHAM BOOK SERVICES LTD.
Isaac Newton Way, Alma Park Industrial Estate
Grantham, Lincolnshire, NG31 9SD, England

Library of Congress Cataloging in Publication Data

Kalergis, Mary Motley
Seen and Heard: Teenagers talk about their lives / photographs and interviews by Mary Motley Kalergis.
p. cm.
ISBN 1-55670-834-3
1. Teenagers—United States—Attitudes. 2. Teenagers—United States—Conduct of life. I. Title.
HQ796.K1867 1998
305.235—dc21 98-7158
CIP

Printed in China

10 9 8 7 6 5 4 3 2 1

Developed and Produced by
VERVE EDITIONS
Burlington, Vermont

To David, my teenage sweetheart and father of our teenagers.

Thanks —

Mary

Foreword

To me, one of the strangest and most terrifying things about being human is the need to come up with an identity. It has always bewildered me, and I can say that even now it's still mostly unresolved. What strikes me about these widely varied interviews with young people is that they all share in common the attempt to balance the shock of what life does to us with our notions of who we would like ourselves to be. In the midst of this struggle I suspect that who we actually are must fall somewhere between the cracks. Now and then we get lucky and capture a true glimpse of ourselves, like lightning in a bottle. It's always a surprise. Amazingly, that truth keeps cropping up in these portraits and leads me to believe that this generation of kids may simply be more honest and courageous than the one I belonged to during my adolescence. Maybe these delirious times have actually forced these kids into a deeper, more sincere confrontation with themselves that somehow eluded us in the post-war fifties. In the 1957 Eisenhower rural California that I came of age in you could not buy a dialogue about identity or the meaning of life on earth. Things were set in granite. There was a tacit agreement that America was on a bright and golden track and you'd better get on board fast or be swept into some evil communist vortex of the soul. A black-and-whiteness existed that was truly scary: Ozzie and Harriet or Lenny Bruce; Perry Como or Little Richard; Walter Cronkite or Jack Kerouac. There was no gray territory to mess around in. No wonder the sixties exploded with such veracity. I'm not a sociologist and, in fact, find the whole pursuit boring and away from the point. If it's possible to strike to the heart of those miraculous seven years between age 13 and 19 it might be the pure animal thrill and terror of facing the unknown. Suddenly, I can see myself moving out into this vast light; being thrust out by nature itself, free falling with no net. I need to come up with something! "Who am I?" As hackneyed and simplistic as this question might sound to us of the dot-com E-mail computer age, it may still remain the most important one we can ever ask — and these young people seem to be asking it for real.

Sam Shepard

Introduction

From the sound bites on the six o'clock news or the stories in the weekly magazines, it's easy to conclude that the next generation is in a downward spiral — more prone to violence and suicidal depression, less ambitious and socially conscious. But what about the "non-news" kids who do their homework, struggle to get along with their families and friends, and tackle the important business of growing up? *Seen and Heard* is a forum where these young people can speak freely about the issues that are most important to them: family, friends, school, work, and their hopes and fears for the future. Some might be surprised at the introspection of these young people. As an interviewer, I'm impressed by their candor and deeply touched by the vulnerability they reveal. As a portrait photographer, I delight in the enthusiastic grace of their collaboration. Having a houseful of my own teenagers and their friends, I've noticed that their boisterous animal vitality often makes adults uneasy. The ages from thirteen through nineteen seem to be the last group unprotected by contemporary political correctness. Under the guise of helping, we adults too often criticize our teens' attitudes and beliefs, and stereotype their appearance and activities. Our desire to both educate and protect them creates a complex mix of emotions as we try to teach them lessons from our own youth. A frequent parents' lament is, "Why won't my kids talk to me?" I asked scores of teenagers about this, and was often greeted with a question in return. "Would you want to talk to a person whose goal in any conversation was to teach you something?" I finally had to admit that, while well-intended, the adult impulse to use every contact with teenagers as a chance to teach a lesson seriously limits communication between the generations. As one teenager in the book says, "Parents can't have a life for you." It takes courage to accept that our children inhabit a dangerous world, and that, despite our best efforts, some of them will be wounded or even killed by their contact with it. The dangers of life will never be completely eliminated. However, an unrecognized danger is that, in our zeal to protect our children from life's risks, we evade the truth about its complexities. When the kids catch us in hypocrisy, our voices lose credibility for moral persuasion. As one young woman observed, "Parents should realize that it's impossible to hide things from kids. They're curious and notice everything. It's really difficult growing up. We need to acknowledge this and talk honestly together. Perfection doesn't inspire trust, honesty does." As a documentary photographer, my intention is to look directly at some part of our common human existence (such as marriage, childbirth, or motherhood) and reflect back my findings through books of portraits and interviews. The writer James Agee describes this kind of documentary work as an examination of "the cruel radiance of what is," rather than the fantasy of what we think should be. This distinction has been my guide. I invite you to set aside expectations and observe the faces and hear the voices of these young human beings as they share the truth about their lives.

— Mary Motley Kalergis

Lisa Briggs

age 13

"If people are really concerned about today's young people, they should stop complaining and get to know them. We're not all slackers. We do have goals and opinions — each one of us different in our own way. The key to understanding is respect."

My older sister has always loved to write plays and I love to perform. It's the best feeling in the world to have an audience's attention, to control their emotions. I also swam competitively for years and there are a lot of similarities between the two. Each meet is like a performance; the minute you get out of the water or the curtain closes, you know whether you've done your personal best. Sometimes the rhythm's right and sometimes it's off. You always try your hardest but you don't always do your best. When I'm on stage or swimming, I'm not shy at all — I give it all I've got.

I was home schooled with my older sisters and our parents never talked down to us. I found it difficult when I started grade school because there was such a gap between the teachers and the kids. My years in public school were not very happy ones. I was used to being treated with respect and encouraged to seek out what I personally enjoyed. I was taught at home to interpret facts and not just recite them. Many of our public schools are designed to churn out factory workers, but the trouble is this country no longer has very many factories. After home schooling, public school felt like prison. Now I go to a small alternative school and it feels much more comfortable. I can work at my own level in each subject.

Having my opinions respected and often acted upon is the greatest gift my parents have given me because I have the self-confidence to make responsible choices. It seems like so many parents don't really listen to their kids. They just tell them how things should be instead of asking how things are. I don't think there's anything wrong with rebelling against authority, because sometimes authority can be wrong. I've never had any reason to rebel myself, because my feelings have always been respected. That doesn't mean my parents never say "no" to me, it's just that when they don't support my wishes, they have a reasonable explanation. My mom doesn't let me get my nose pierced, not because she doesn't like it, but because it might hurt my goals of modeling or acting. It's like even when they say "no", they're always on my side. My father says when I do well, he's happy for me, but he doesn't take pride in my accomplishments, because they're mine, not his. They don't act like they own us.

There's a huge difference between supporting a child's needs and spoiling a child. If you buy them things to quiet their whining, it's just buying them off. When parents give their kids gifts and privileges without acknowledging the reason they might want those things, the gesture has little value. It's as important to understand why your children want something as what your kids want because it gives them the message that their thoughts have worth, and makes them feel understood. Without understanding, there's not much closeness. Because my parents have always understood me, it's impossible for me to lie to them.

If people are really concerned about today's young people, they should stop complaining and get to know them. We're not all slackers. We do have goals and opinions — each one of us different in our own way. The key to understanding is respect. When you understand people's differences, there's more respect in the family, and that makes for a stronger community.

Aaron Skoglund

age 17

"Even though parents and teachers should share all their knowledge with their kids, they shouldn't necessarily expect them to accept it. They shouldn't expect them to be just like them. People should respect each other because of, not in spite of, their differences."

My parents divorced when I was in eighth grade. It hurt, but it was probably the best thing that ever happened to me. I feel like it was a trauma that brought out my potential. Right after my dad left, I got really depressed. I couldn't bring myself to talk to my mom about it. It's like it was important for me to feel totally alone in order to get to know myself. Now I have a close relationship with both of my parents and I appreciate it much more than I could if I hadn't had that time of feeling totally isolated.

My dad's a dreamer and hasn't always been successful in business, but his belief in things you can't prove has been an inspiration to me. The day of my Bar Mitzvah was an awesome experience. While I was reading from the Torah, my dad was just weeping and it struck me how much more there is to life than we normally see. It was a very spiritual moment when I realized how much I don't know. I was just standing there, a little basketball player with short hair, in awe of how much knowledge is out there for the taking. At thirteen I realized there is something very real surrounding all the ritual.

When I was a baby, I loved music so much. Nothing made me happier. I was always in chorus in school until I got really depressed after my parents' divorce. My chorus teacher really tried to help me out, but I felt like I had to withdraw from everybody and everything. All I did the year I turned fourteen is listen to music. My mom got me a guitar during the summer before tenth grade. I took lessons and started playing all the time. Before I had my guitar I used to write a lot of written confusion, but the rhythm of the music kinda organized my thoughts and now I write songs and poetry. In Israel this summer I took a music workshop that really taught me to express myself. I've been experimenting with all different styles of music — everything from Folk to Rap. Music is definitely my way of communicating with others. It's a way of understanding the rhythms of nature; its cycles and seasons, the rhythm of life. It's a universal language that speaks to all cultures.

When adults say my ideals of equality are not realistic, I say that their so-called realism is really pessimism. When people demand proof, I know that a lot of truth comes from the heart and is beyond explaining. The best way to learn anything is to examine it from all sides. Following your heart isn't necessarily doing what you want. In fact, the right thing isn't always the easy thing. It takes a lot of courage to feed your soul and not your ego.

Even though parents and teachers should share all their knowledge with their kids, they shouldn't necessarily expect them to accept it. They shouldn't expect them to be just like them. People should respect each other because of, not in spite of, their differences. My dream is to become a teacher and teach kids just like a good parent raises a child — with love and acceptance. So far my parents have been my most valuable teachers, because they taught me how to love.

Schuyler Fisk

age 14

"My parents have always cared about what I think and how I feel and that's probably why I feel the same way about them. It's really hard for kids to get along with their parents if their mom and dad can't get along with each other."

Growing up on movie sets didn't seem strange at all. I guess I thought that tons of people, cameras, and cables was normal. It seemed perfectly normal to me. When I started first grade, I remember people asking me, "Isn't it weird that your mom's a movie star?" I felt defensive, like maybe that was some sort of insult. I have one friend that always introduced me as Sissy Spacek's daughter. She finally got over it and now introduces me by my own name. When we're in New York or L.A., I get a sense of her celebrity, but in the town where we live, she's a part of the community. To me, she's Mom.

When she was making a movie, I'd make friends with the kid actors on the set. In a lot of her films, I'd be an extra if there were parts for children, but after a while, I started thinking, "Hey, if they have speaking roles, why can't I?" She didn't want me to get in the business when I was so young, so I continued to perform in school plays and theater groups. One day, out of the blue, we got a call from one of Mom's old friends, who was directing the movie *Babysitter's Club*. She asked if I was into acting, and Mom couldn't deny that I was. They were looking for a girl to play Christie, so we sent them a tape of me reading for the part. I wasn't even nervous, because I didn't think I'd get the lead role and I don't think my mom thought I would either, or she probably wouldn't have let me try out! I think the whole family was shocked when I got the part. I loved the whole experience of making the movie, but keeping up with my school work was really hard. Even my old friends back at home treated me differently after I made *Babysitter's Club*. No one was like, "That's so cool, you were in a movie!" Instead, they were like, "Oh, she's in that baby movie." Of course, girls tend to be kinda mean in sixth grade, no matter what you do or who you are.

When I'm in a movie, I get to tap into both my dad's experience as a director and my mom's experience as an actor. I really admire both of my parents. I really look up to them and I know that a lot of my friends don't feel that way about their parents. I feel like I'm really connected to them, like we're alike, but some of my friends almost feel like total strangers with their family. My parents have always cared about what I think and how I feel and that's probably why I feel the same way about them. It's really hard for kids to get along with their parents if their mom and dad can't get along with each other. I assume that when I grow up, I'll be in the film business, get married, and have a couple of kids. I'll pretty much have the same life I do now, except this time I'll be the mom!

This was my first year of high school and I loved it. Kids are more accepting and supportive. The girls aren't so into cliques and it's much more possible to be friends with boys. They aren't so immature anymore, making fart jokes or tipping over their chairs in class. You can talk to the same boys that a year ago wouldn't have been able to carry on a serious conversation. Everyone I know hated eighth grade. It's cliquish and the homework is overwhelming. One thing I really loved about being a freshman this year is there were so many older kids to look up to. It's inspiring to me. It makes everything seem like it has more purpose when there are certain people to look up to.

Aviva Dove-Viebahn

age 14

"Those little blocks that you have to check on applications, to identify your race, make me really mad. Sometimes I check 'other,' if that's an option. If not, I'll check 'black,' since a majority of the people in this country are white, so I might as well balance things out! Funnily enough, having a black mother and a white father has made the subject of race almost a non-issue in our house."

I didn't start school as a child prodigy. I mean, when I started kindergarten, I knew the alphabet, but I didn't know how to read or write. Pretty soon after I started school, I could easily figure out what the teachers wanted on a test, so it wasn't very hard for me to make good grades. I'd probably be a lot smarter, or at least know a lot more, if I couldn't figure out what I needed to know and what I could just skip over and ignore.

I was in the gifted program in middle school and I took this talent search test for a summer program called CTY (Center for Talented Youth). I got in and went to Goucher College in Baltimore during the summer, for a three week course on the Renaissance. I guess that program must have given PEG (Program for the Exceptionally Gifted) at Mary Baldwin College my name and address, because I got an application in the mail. At first, the idea of skipping high school seemed like a stupid idea, but when I came here and visited the campus, I just loved the place right away and I got intrigued by the possibilities of being in such an intellectually challenging environment. The first thing they told us when we came here was that you don't have to ask permission to go to the bathroom. Fresh from eighth grade, that seemed like a wonderful freedom!

One of my favorite things about being here is I get to make friends with people from different places. I've traveled so much with my parents, that I don't even notice accents. My dad is German, and I can't even hear his accent — he just sounds like my dad! I don't even remember my first trip abroad, and can't count how many times I've been to Europe. Being on campus seems like traveling to a lot of different places at once, since the students are from all over. I love the sense of community and all the activity on dorm. Being an only child, with both parents avid readers and writers, things were pretty quiet at home. I used to love being home alone, but now it seems eerily quiet. We hardly ever turned on the TV, and that's a big difference between me and a lot of my friends here at the college, who must have spent a good many hours every week watching *MTV*, because they know all the lyrics and every time it's on in the dorm, everyone has seen the video before — except me, who knows very little about popular music. My parents gave me a love of classical music and opera. I'm taking voice lessons and working on an aria from *The Marriage of Figaro*. Mozart is one of my favorite composers.

I really feel like a citizen of the world more than an American. I feel just as German as I do American. Those little blocks that you have to check on applications, to identify your race, make me really mad. Sometimes I check "other," if that's an option. If not, I'll check "black," since a majority of the people in this country are white, so I might as well balance things out! Funnily enough, having a black mother and a white father has made the subject of race almost a non-issue in our house.

I remember thinking in a daydream, before I had even heard of the PEG program, "Wouldn't it be really great if I could graduate from college by the time I was eighteen?" I'd been writing this science fiction story about this fourteen-year-old girl in a Star Fleet Academy, which is like a military college in the television show *Star Trek*, and even though she's young, she can go through the paces.

Program
for
Exceptionally
Gifted
South Bailey
Residence Hall

NIKE NATIONAL PREP
CHAMPIONSHIP
LAS VEGAS NEVADA
19
96

Hajj Malik Turner

age 17

"When I think of my five closest friends, I'm the only one who lives in a family with both parents. When I think of all the influence my dad has had on my daily life, it's hard to imagine who I'd be if he wasn't around. It's hard enough to be a mother, let alone a mother and a father."

Having my dad be dean of African-American Affairs has definitely raised my consciousness about race. He always made sure we learned our black history. Like most kids my age, I read the sports and the funnies in the paper, but I also read the rest of it as well. Both my parents always had us reading a lot, especially books by African-American authors. I loved the Walter D. Myers books about growing up and I'm a big fan of the Easy Rollins mysteries. The stuff they have us reading at school really doesn't fit my taste. I like the classes where the students can get involved in the discussion. I hate English this year because the teacher's way is the only way and I think when you read books, there's different ways to interpret them.

All the books we read in school are about white people and then we're supposed to respond to them just like some esteemed critic, whether you agree or not. We're reading *Wuthering Heights* right now. I hate that book! I can't stand Heathcliff or Kathy! It's hard for me to believe that any kid my age would enjoy that story. I can never just say, "Yes, Ma'am" or "no, Sir" if I think I have a valid point. I can be pretty argumentative. I have a really strong sense of fairness and it's hard for me to ignore something if it is just plain wrong.

I don't think the teachers should be disrespectful to the students, but it goes both ways. My dad's job is to be an advocate for minority students at the university, so that's probably where I get a sense of fairness that won't back down. When I think of my five closest friends, I'm the only one who lives in a family with both parents. When I think of all the influence my dad has had on my daily life, it's hard to imagine who I'd be if he wasn't around. It's hard enough to be a mother, let alone a mother and a father.

This country is very much a white culture, but each individual can build or break down their own boundaries. My family lives in a mostly white neighborhood, but socially we tend to be with other people of color. I've never dated a white girl, not because I think there's anything wrong with it, but I tell people straight up, it's not racist, it's just being attracted to women who look like the role models I was raised with. My own mother is the type of woman that I would like to be with some day, not some blond movie star. It bothers me that so many black men go and get a white girlfriend as soon as they become rich or famous. I see some people who try to avoid all white people, but you're just punishing yourself with those limitations. It's a big world of all colors out there and you shouldn't limit your expectations.

That doesn't mean that you don't get hit with some unfair assumptions when you're a young black man, especially a tall one! I remember one time when me and a friend of mine were out trying to find some party. He rolled down the window and said, "Excuse me, could you..." and the lady just ran across the street. We laughed about it at the time, but later on, at home alone, it seemed more sad than funny. I notice when someone reaches over and locks their door when I walk by. One time I was in a store, and an undercover guy was following me around, trying to act all cool and casual. In his pressed jeans and tucked-in shirt, he might as well have Undercover Agent printed on his shirt! It's really kind of insulting.

Malcolm X is hero of mine. I really admire how he built up a belief in black power, yet after he went to the nation of Islam, he recanted all his negative feelings about whites. You've got to be really strong to make a stand, then admit your mistakes. His pilgrimage to Mecca gave him the strength. Hajj means pilgrimage and Malik means king. My name, Hajj Malik, is Malcolm's Muslim name, and I'm proud to have it. The thing I hold closest to my heart is my family. My parents are my biggest heroes and my big brother and sister are my most important role models.

Marco Marraccini

age 19

"If I have any heroes, other than Michael Jordan, who is the epitome of talent and hard work, it's my own family that inspires me. Both of my parents have worked long and hard for everything we have and because I respect them so much, I want them to be proud of me."

My learning disabilities started showing up by second grade. I've always had a lot of motivation to do well, unlike most of the other students in the special resources classes. It never occurred to me that I wouldn't go on to college. It might take me much longer to get my work done, but I won't quit until I know I've done my best. When I got to high school I had a teacher who really encouraged me when I needed it most. I felt compelled to get straight As, but my reading is so slow and my spelling so bad, I had to spend much more time on my class work than anyone else. A lot of kids in my situation decide they really don't care about school, but I couldn't stop caring. I've developed a lot of skills to overcome my slowness, but I still need to take un-timed tests and I'd never be able to take in lectures at the university without note takers. By the time I've written down what the professor has said, I'm three new ideas behind. Books on tape help, too. Even though they're slow, it's faster for me to listen than it is to read. Now that I'm studying architecture, I'm not any slower than anyone else because the work is project oriented.

It's great to find a place where I'm playing on a level playing field. Everyone complains about how many hours they have to put into their work, but to me it's no different than what I've been doing all along. It's no lucky accident that I'm in Architecture. I purposely chose it because I could play to my strengths instead of weaknesses. It's no surprise that I like it very much, because it is a place where my abilities are as strong as anyone else's. I've had to be supremely organized to get to where I am now and it's starting to really pay off.

College has been a great experience for me because I'm surrounded by people who are as ambitious and hardworking as I am. At the same time there seems to be less peer pressure to conform. It's been a revelation to me that I'm just as smart as the other kids here. It's really boosted my self-confidence in the future. Back in grade school and high school I used to think I probably wasn't as smart as the average student. Even though I made good grades, I knew that I had to work twice as long to get them. Now I don't have to work much harder than anyone else to get good grades. Once I'm out of the academic world, I shouldn't need much remedial help.

My teen years have been much more enjoyable in the late teens. Early adolescence is rough. You feel awkward in your own body and school just keeps piling on more and more work. Girls your age don't pay any attention to you because they like the older boys. Everyone is starting to experiment with smoking and drinking and even if you feel far from ready to try those things, you feel a lot of pressure to go along. I've always been like an adult in a little kid's body, so it's a relief to finally be old enough to not feel old beyond my years.

If I have any heroes, other than Michael Jordan, who is the epitome of talent and hard work, it's my own family that inspires me. My grandmother always wanted to go to college, but after her husband died, she worked long hours to put my dad through school. Both of my parents have worked long and hard for everything we have and because I respect them so much, I want them to be proud of me. But I can honestly say that my own hard work is something that I'm driven to do more than something I do for my parents. One reason my parents have been successful is they're doing what they love to do. My definition of success is loving your work. One major problem with America is most people just think of a job as a way to make money. It should be more than that. It's certainly easier to work hard at something you love to do and I'm proof that hard work pays off. Even if financial success doesn't come, you'll be doing what you love. I'm going to work hard at what I like to do and be the Michael Jordan of my own career, whatever that may ultimately be.

Lewis Lamb

age 15

"My brother and I will probably raise our own kids right here on this farm one day. I don't even daydream about leaving here, except to go to college and then I'd bring everything I learned right back home. My girlfriend comes from a dairy farming family, so she understands all the hours I have to put into the place. Whoever I marry one day would have to accept this way of life."

My family has worked this farm since long before I was born. When I was about nine I started having chores with the livestock. I'm in charge of all the babies from the time we take them off their mamas until they're turned out to pasture. I've been in 4-H since I was a little kid and I still enjoy it, raising up a little baby calf. I really like their attitudes — no matter what you've done to them the day before, they're always glad to see you coming.

When my brother and I play football in the fall, our cousin takes over our chores and then when he has wrestling in the winter, we take over for him, so it works out pretty good. We alternate between feeding and cleaning the barn on the weekends. Most of my friends at school do farm work with their family, so my life doesn't seem too unusual. In the summer I spend a lot of my time keeping the grass mowed down and rotating the cows from pasture to pasture.

I've always wanted to go to college and learn about animal medicine and agriculture. My older brother is interested in the mechanical side of farming. He's always working on the trucks and tractors, where I'm more concerned with the livestock. Ever since he was a little kid, he's always liked to take stuff apart and ever since I was small, I've always liked to play with the calves. I think we'll be a good team one day just like my dad and his brother. My uncle likes to look after the crops and the tractors while my daddy likes to take care of the cows.

My older sister helps out with the cooking and the laundry with my mom. Even though she's planning on going to college, she plans on staying in Madison County, near the family farm. Our whole family has always pitched in together — that's the way it has to be to run a family farm. Every morning my grandma helps my daddy feed the calves and she does all the cooking for everyone when school is out.

My brother and I will probably raise our own kids right here on this farm one day. I don't even daydream about leaving here, except to go to college and then I'd bring everything I learned right back home. Small dairy farms are being run out by big business and the only way for our family farm to survive is to learn how to grow and keep up with technology. If you don't know anything about computers you won't last long nowadays. My girlfriend comes from a dairy farming family, so she understands all the hours I have to put into the place. Whoever I marry one day would have to accept this way of life. My mom doesn't work in the barns, but she likes to ride with Daddy when he checks on the herds that are away from the farm and she always has dinner waiting for us. My grandma sews beautiful quilts and works as hard as any man outside on the place. The men and women in this family really work together. Everyone counts on one another.

SELECT SIRES

Whore-Hey
A DAY AT THE BEACH...
NEW YORK
THE BIG APPLE
Bob Marley

Ryan Malbon

age 17

"I have very little self-respect right now. When your own mom thinks you're a jerk, it makes it hard. She thinks I'm the biggest fuck-up in the world, but I'm her fuck-up, she gave birth to me."

My home life in junior high was way less than fun. My parents were separated and I was living with my mom. She kicked me out of the house when I was thirteen. I was her first born, the oldest of four kids, and everything with me was new to her. She had no idea how to deal with a boy that age. She thinks I'm the biggest fuck-up in the world, but I'm her fuck-up, she gave birth to me. When I was a little kid, my mom was the greatest, but when I got older and wanted more freedom, it seems like we became enemies. I've always wanted more freedom than I have and always will, I think. By the time I was twelve, I didn't want to ride my bike at all, I wanted to drive. I stole my parents' car lots of times. It's like I just didn't care about the consequences, I just did things on impulse. Parents always say, "Hey, we were there, we were teenagers once." But almost everyone grows up to be just like their parents, and once that happens, they forget what it's like to be a kid. When their kids become teenagers, they're lost, because they've forgotten what it's like to feel so restricted. And when you have your freedom taken totally away, it's the worst. My mom's parents were very strict, her dad was military and that was just the way she learned. She learned how to kick butt. When she'd punish me by grounding me, it would make me want to do the same thing again, just to get back at her. It's the only offense you have. Parents forget how petrified we are of making them angry or disappointing them. It makes them hard to talk to.

I have very little self-respect right now. When your own mom thinks you're a jerk, it makes it hard. Giving your children respect is good. You're much more likely to get it back, because it goes both ways. Both my mom and my grandfather go through my stuff, trying to find anything they don't want me to have. To me, it's wrong to treat someone that way. It's just plain disrespectful.

Kids don't have a lot of respect for the government because the government doesn't give us much respect. Look at the twenty-one-year-old drinking age. I mean, come on — I can take a bullet for my country, sign a legal contract or get married, but I can't have a beer? That's ridiculous, and we know it. The "war on drugs" is a joke — a waste of taxpayers' money. Keeping them illegal just increases crime, by making them more expensive and making millions of recreational users criminal. Making it illegal for kids under eighteen to buy cigarettes will only make them more desirable. I've been to court twice for illegal possession of tobacco. That's just plain police harassment.

When I had just started ninth grade, my mom was out of town and I was supposed to be staying with my grandparents. I had a huge party at her house every night. I cleaned up the place really well, but she figured it out and told me I wasn't welcome to stay there anymore. My grandparents were mad at me, too, because I lied to them, but they still offered me a place to stay. My dad moved back in and wanted to get the family back together, so I moved back home a few months later, but I wasn't that happy about it because I was still mad at my mom. As soon as they left town, I did the same thing again. So she did the same thing, too and kicked me out again. I stayed at friends' houses, wearing the same clothes everyday. This time my grandparents were so mad at being lied to again, that they wouldn't take me back, so I moved in with my dad's father, which my parents really didn't like at all, because his home life is more than a little whacked. His wife is a twenty-seven-year-old crack addict. There's bullet holes all over the house. It's a crazy scene. She acts like my friend, but she's two-faced. I tell her things, then when she wants something from my grandfather, she'll tell him things I told her in confidence. I've learned to keep quiet. He couldn't get me out of bed one morning to go to school, so he threw a bucket of water on me and I called him an asshole. He said, "If you think I'm an asshole, pack your stuff and get out." I tried to take it back, but he said go. I stayed with my dad in his camper at the marina. He'd moved out of the house again because he and my mom were fightin'.

After a while, he moved back in with Mom and he wanted me to come with him, so I did. But it was still like camping out. I stayed on the couch for about three months, but that got old, feelin' like a visitor in my parents' house. My mom and me fought all the time. One day she swung at me and I laughed at her, which really set her off, so I started to run. She's chasing me around the kitchen table, yelling at me to get out. I heard her on the phone with my dad, saying I was the one cussing and swinging punches. I just sat in the driveway and cried, because I knew he would always take her side. I stayed with friends for a few days until I got the nerve to call my dad. He told me to have a nice life, that he'd had it with me. I was in the wrong, I won't deny that, but so was she. We both messed up. My mom and I still don't get along that good, but I love my dad to death. I moved back in with his dad and after a while, I dropped out of school.

I'd been sleepin' through most of my classes anyway. It's boring to me and homework is just stupid busy work. Right now I'm kinda wishin' that I stayed in school, but I pretty much screwed it for myself. I don't think I could stand having to repeat an extra year. I'm a night person, so maybe I could do better in night school. At least I'd have a chance of staying awake.

My dad has come around to realize that my mom exaggerates and he's back on my side again. I work for him down at the marina. He treats me like a friend. I love it, though sometimes it's hard because I work for him, and I'm his son, so sometimes it gets mixed up. My sister gets along with my mom pretty good. I guess it's a mother/daughter thing. My two little brothers are the noise boys. They really look up to me but it's hard for me to spend much time with them because I can't get along with my mom and they are so noisy, they give me a headache. I don't think my sister likes me very much. She thinks I'm the cause of all the problems in the family. Maybe she'll come to understand how I feel about things when she gets a little older.

I have a hard time sleeping at night. I lie awake and wonder about what I'm going to do with my life. Now I'm getting a little bit scared. I've got to figure out something. I can't work at the marina for the rest of my life. I dock boats, paint boats, sand boats. This winter I started driving the forklift. I've been working there for four years and even though I like riding in boats and fishing, I hate 'em. I'm tired of them. It's a job to me. I love the ocean. I love seafood and surfing and fishing offshore. When I die, I want my ashes to be buried at sea. I never get tired of just sitting on the beach and watching the water. Mother Nature calms me.

I don't think there is a God, because if there was, He wouldn't let all the bad stuff happen to people that deserve better. I believe in survival of the fittest. Poverty makes people resort to crime. People have to make it somehow. I don't believe in the Golden Rule. If you see something you want, you take it. If I leave my stuff lying around, I don't expect it to be there for me when I get back. I might not like it, but I wouldn't be surprised. Shoplifting isn't a crime unless you get caught. I have to take advantage of every situation that I'm in. If I don't know you, my conscience doesn't bother me, but I'd never steal from someone I know, even if I didn't like them. I used to feel guilty when I'd sneak my dad's cigarettes. If someone takes something from me, I'd be real mad, but then I'd have to stop and think, "I'd probably do the same thing" — so how mad can I be? Sometimes when I'm lying in bed at night, I think I need to think of some get-rich-quick scheme, but then I think how proud of myself I'd be if I went to college and got some job behind a desk, and make two-hundred grand a year. It's survival of the fittest and I have to figure out what to do. I feel like I'm sixteen, going on twenty-five.

ADDY
estro
WU-TANG
CLAN
LM

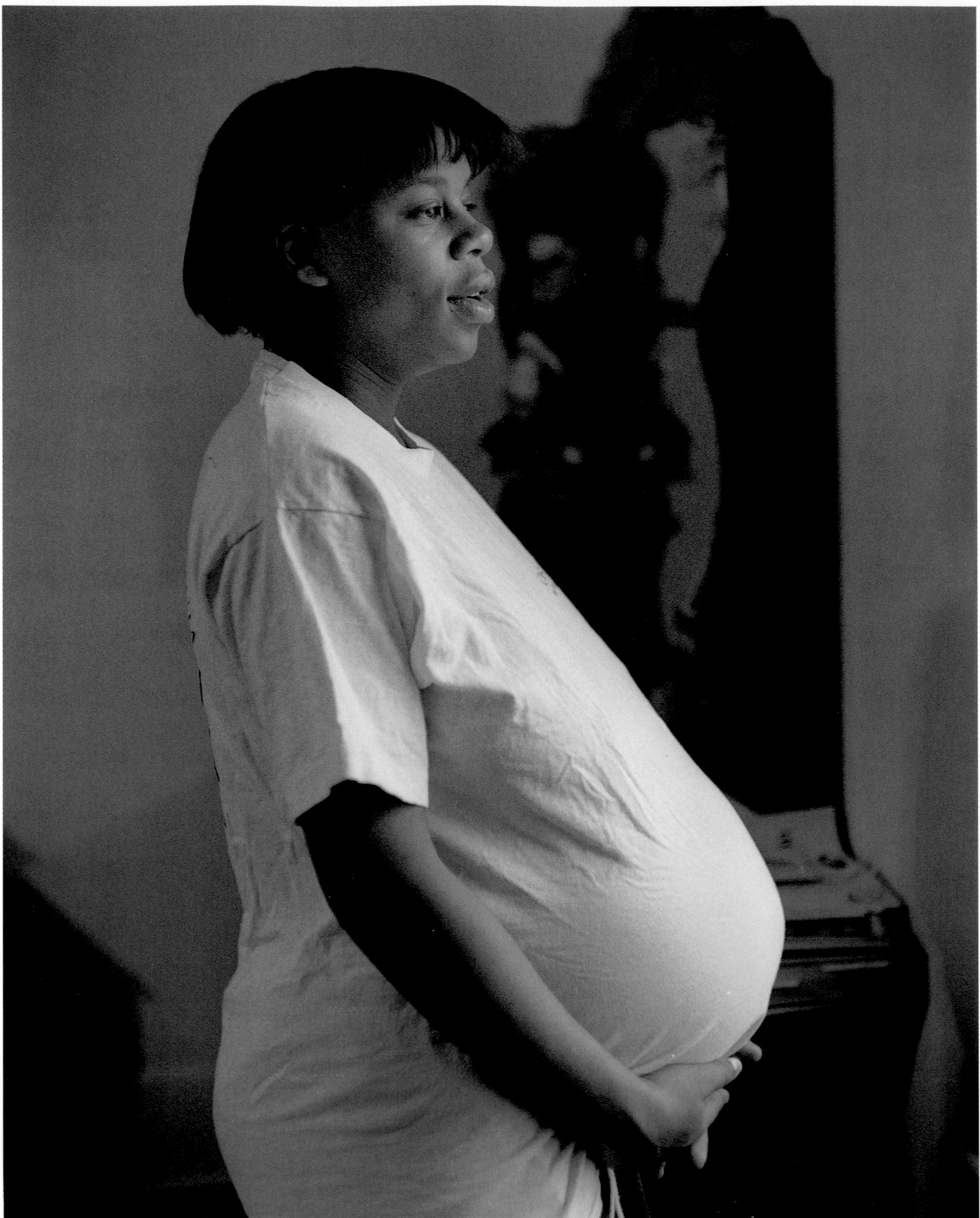

Sabrina Allen

age 17

"I want to tell young girls out there who want to get a baby that it's not pretty and it doesn't make you grown. When I was chillin' with my boyfriend, I felt like a grown woman, but when I found out I was pregnant, I really needed my mom."

I always got good grades until high school, then I guess I got around the wrong crowd and I started skipping all my classes. Kids at my high school like to hang out instead of going to class. I got the stupid idea that it wasn't cool to make good grades. I got a boyfriend that was older than me and I wanted to be all grown-up. When we first started having sex, I was worried about getting pregnant, but it seems like after a while I just stopped worrying about it. I think I just blocked it out, thinking it couldn't happen to me. I want to tell young girls out there who want to get a baby that it's not pretty and it doesn't make you grown. It makes you feel low. I felt like a failure when I found out it could happen to me — in fact, it had! I didn't even want to go out of the house for the longest time, but my mom was really there for me then and helped me through it. I was just so shocked. When I was chillin' with my boyfriend, I felt like a grown woman but when I found out I was pregnant, I really needed my mom. If anyone my age asks me for advice, I'd say "Listen to your mom." That would be the first thing out of my mouth. Nobody loves you more or longer. They know more than you. I thought it was cool to hang, smoking weed and having sex, but it wasn't. They say "Live and learn," and I learned the hard way. I stayed out late at night. Sometimes I didn't come home for days. Whenever I did go to school, I'd just get suspended for causing trouble. I had always been the quiet type but now I was starting fights. It seemed like I didn't care about anything. I used to go pick on the nerdy kids, because I wasn't a nerd anymore. Yeah, real cool — I failed ninth grade.

When my boyfriend and I made a baby, I was afraid to tell my mom, even though she was always wonderful to me (or maybe because she was always so nice). Before I got to high school, we could talk about anything, but then I developed an attitude and she couldn't tell me nothing. She would try to tell me right from wrong and I just wouldn't listen. I would just be silent, just close her out. When she found out about the pregnancy and asked me what I wanted to do, I just kept saying "I don't know, I just don't know." When she told me she'd help me out as much as she could, I decided to raise the baby myself — with my mother's help. And to think, I used to want to be a grown-up. I've had to think about the future since I got pregnant and I've already made some plans. I'm going to take my GED after the baby is born and then take cosmetology classes. I've always been good at working with hair and I hope to work at my aunt's beauty salon.

Teenagers care more about what their friends think and say than what their parents want. Peer pressure is everything and that's why it's important not to hang around with the wrong crowd. I chose an older crowd to hang with because I wanted to feel grown. Now my childhood is gone and I regret it. I learned a lot but it cost a lot.

Patrice and Norma Jane Mejias

age 16

Norma Jane: "I feel every person gets a life and you have to learn to accept whatever you get, no matter what it is. I believe I'm doing exactly what I'm supposed to be doing in this life time." Patrice: "I wrote a paper on *Great Expectations* in school – about how suffering can lead to enlightenment. Probably on some level, I learned that lesson more from my sister than Dickens."

PATRICE: When I started walking and Janie couldn't, I remember wondering why, but her handicaps were never that big a deal for us, because that's the way it's always been. Just like being twins, we don't know any other way of being.

NORMA JANE: I sometimes wonder what it would be like if Patrice had the cerebral palsy and I was like her, but I just can't picture her having the same disability I do and me being able to walk, because I'm just accustomed to things being the way they are.

PATRICE: I have sometimes wondered what it would be like for us if I was the twin with the disability, but more often I think about how it might be if neither one of us had handicaps. I don't think I am as accepting as Janie. I have more anger about her (medical problems) because I believe they could have been prevented by the doctors if they had done a better job.

NORMA JANE: I agree, yet at the same time I feel every person gets a life and you have to learn to accept whatever you get, no matter what it is. I have to believe in reincarnation and I could come back as the President one day! Who knows, maybe in my last life I was rich and beautiful and this time around I've got different stuff to learn. To become a well rounded spirit, God puts you in a body and you have to accept your own individual story for that lifetime. If you die young, that's just the cards you were dealt that time around. That's the only way I can explain to myself why some people get cancer at five and die. Who knows? Maybe I'll be a dancer or a gymnast in my next life. That's how I've come to terms with my circumstances. I believe I'm doing exactly what I'm supposed to be doing in this lifetime.

PATRICE: I wrote a paper on *Great Expectations* in school about how suffering can lead to enlightenment. Probably on some level, I learned that lesson more from my sister than Dickens. I definitely admire her courage and acceptance. These are things we never talk about, but they're part of our daily lives. We've studied Buddhism in school, and it sounds very much like Janie's philosophy. I had no idea that she was so wise!

NORMA JANE: I don't know anything about Buddhism. I kinda just made this stuff up as I went along. My family's not really into religion. I mean, we believe in God, of course, but I just invented my own religion on my own. I had no idea these ideas were thousands of years old. Maybe I was a Buddhist in my last life and just don't remember! The reason we can't remember our past lives is we'd always be looking back instead of moving forward and learning the lessons we need to learn in this lifetime.

PATRICE: Our generation is the first one where middle class girls just assume, like boys, that we'll have to earn a living. I don't know anyone who assumes they'll be able to be supported on their husband's one income.

NORMA JANE: Look at TV nowadays. There's no more full-time housewives. Florence Henderson would have to go to work after she made the breakfast today.

PATRICE: I'll probably get married and have kids one day, but I know how much my brother's college tuition costs, so I can't imagine that I won't have to go to work, too.

Hawaiian Surf

Matt & Beau Mclaughlin

age 13 & 15

Beau: "Our mom's been real sick with cancer, and we haven't even talked about that. We both tend to talk to our friends before we'd talk to each other." Matt: "Sometimes it just feels like it makes things even more complicated to talk to your family."

BEAU: I'm in high school, and Matt's still in junior high, and we both tend to hang out with friends from school, so we're in different groups.

MATT: We don't talk much about things that are bothering us. We kind of keep it to ourselves.

BEAU: Our mom's been real sick with cancer, and we haven't even talked about that. We both tend to talk to our friends before we'd talk to each other.

MATT: Sometimes it just feels like it makes things even more complicated to talk to your family.

BEAU: I like to keep busy more than sit around and talk about things anyway. I've been playing ice hockey since I was six and little league for almost as long.

MATT: Since I was always at either hockey or baseball practice when I was really small, I just naturally got interested and started playing. Every now and then it bothers me that since Beau is older than me, he's always a couple of years ahead of me competitively and I wish I could be better than him at something. Since he's always going to be older than me, it seems a little bit unfair — like I can never catch up to his level. I don't play baseball anymore and I've switched from ice hockey to roller hockey, so we do even less together now. Beau's definitely more committed to his sports than I am. It's like he's driven by something I don't understand.

BEAU: You see that a lot in families. We have cousins like us. The oldest kid plays college football and is going to try out for the Eagles, while his younger brother is a great athlete, but he doesn't have the drive to do much with it. I'm probably going off to boarding school next year, to get better prepared for college, as well as play a much higher level of hockey.

MATT: Beau's definitely the competitive one while I'm more laid back. He picks on me and I turn around and pick on my little sister. Then he comes down on me even harder, because he's real protective of our sister! When he goes away this fall, I kinda like the idea of not having to share a room and am looking forward to being the oldest for a while.

BEAU: I want to go real bad, but at the same time, I know I might get homesick way up there. Also, with my mom being so sick, it makes me more nervous to leave home. She's insisting that I go, because she knows it's something I've wanted to do for a while, but the timing's kind of hard right now.

MATT: It seems like I have to share my stuff with Beau more than he has to share his stuff with me.

BEAU: Yeah, it's great being a big brother because you always have someone to pick on. I hate it when he wears my clothes. Sometimes I wear his stuff, just to prove I can when I want to — at least when my mom's not home. If she is, she'll make me take it off.

MATT: She's been so sick lately, we try not to drag her into our mess. When they told us she had a brain tumor, I wasn't even that shocked, because I was worried that something was pretty wrong.

BEAU: We both had been worrying about her, but we never talked about it. It's like we didn't want to say the words. You never think anything like that could happen to your family, but it's just there...

MATT:...and it doesn't go away when you wake up.

Emily Leonard

age 16

"Animals are just there for you in the most wonderful way. The unconditional love they offer is one of the finest things there is. Sometimes I think human families would be a lot better off if we were more like them."

There's a lot of truth to the expression that a dog is man's best friend. Animals are just there for you in the most wonderful way. The unconditional love they offer is one of the finest things there is. They know things beyond the communication of words. I find their behavior endlessly fascinating. The large mammal house here at the zoo is a lot of backbreaking work. We shovel 5,000 pounds of manure a day, but it's worth it to get to know the animals. Sometimes I think human families would be a lot better off if we were more like the elephants.

Loving animals is the easiest thing in the world for me. Going to school is kind of tough. I have a reading disorder that makes it really difficult for me to comprehend what is written on the page. It wasn't discovered until junior high, so for many years, schoolwork was really a struggle. Things went from bad to worse for a while because when they put me in the Chapter One program, I got really bored in most of the classes because my problem was reading comprehension, not intelligence. In fact, I tested way above my grade level in math, whereas I tested way below my grade level in reading. Most of the kids in those classes had really bad behavior problems and the teachers had to spend most of their time correcting people. In eighth grade I got straight As, which was really ridiculous, because I didn't learn a thing. The next year I just stopped doing any work at all because I had no respect for a system that was just a complete waste of time. My sophomore year, I was tested for ADD (Attention Deficit Disorder) and learning disorders and that ended up getting me a prescription for Ritalin, which has helped me stay focused to get my work done.

I think the tester's encouragement about my intelligence helped me as much as the medication. I realized that I had subconsciously felt crappy about myself, or at least about my learning problems, and I really didn't like not caring. It was the only way I could allow myself to feel because caring and failing so miserably was just too painful. I'm trying really hard to pull my grades up, and the Ritalin has helped me have some success. Before I had the medication, every time someone got up to sharpen a pencil or coughed, I'd totally loose my concentration. I've seen some kids use their ADD diagnosis as an excuse to screw up, so even though putting a name to things can be helpful to understanding and dealing with a problem, you've got to be careful to not use it as a crutch.

I've always pretty much kept my feelings to myself. None of my friends know that I need to take Ritalin. I was in a car accident last September with my best friend, the only one I really ever confided in, and she was killed. We knew everything about each other and had a lot of plans. I still sort of run things by her in my mind, though, of course, she can't talk back. I think the animals are the only ones I really share my truest feelings with right now.

Tenth grade year didn't get off to a very good start, losing my best friend the first week of school. I had enough trouble concentrating before she died. I had to go to summer school this summer, because school just seemed irrelevant compared to the sadness I was feeling last year. The school sent in these grief counselors to talk to us after Nat died, but they had no idea what was going on. A counselor asked me when I found out about Nat's death, and looked shocked when I told her Nat died in my arms. I found it more irritating than comforting to have to talk about Natalie with these so-called experts. Sometimes grown-ups like to put labels on us. "She's ADD" or "she's grief-stricken." But people are much more complicated than you can define in a label.

Rosaura Aguirre

age 18

"One of my favorite things about this country is that there are so many different kinds of people. In Mexico, you only see the Spanish-speaking people. We have no word in my language for teenager."

I left Mexico two years ago. My father took the opportunity when there was the amnesty for his family to come to him in America. He picks the harvest. My mother is sad because she misses her mother and grandmother back in Mexico. The women in Mexican families are very, very close and it gives her a lot of pain to be far away. She works in the lumber yard every day but, her English is still not so good because she's not in school like me and my little brother and sisters.

I go to the high school and it was very hard at first because I could not understand what people were saying. When I try to speak, the people would all laugh at me and I start to think maybe I don't want to go to school anymore. It gave me the most terrible feeling to be so alone when I was there. I just want to stay inside the house with my family. For one month, I would not go to school. They would ask me questions that I didn't understand, like "Do you like the boys?" and I always try to be nice and say "Yes!" and they all laugh at me. It makes me feel so bad. But I'm not the kind of person to just give up, so I go to class and say, "I can do this thing." I like very much America and I know I have to learn the English to get a good job, so I have to be brave and go to school, even though I was very scared at first. Now I am very happy because I can understand and take care of myself. I have friends now and that makes things better. In the Mexican house, the oldest daughter takes care of everyone and I'm the same way at school and people like that. I come home from school and cook the dinner every day. I look out for people wherever I go.

There was a girl at school who tried to take my money. She pulls my hair and pushes me and says, "Give me your money." I said, "No! I only give my money to my mother. You can't have it." I tell her not to fight, that she can get in big trouble and it is better to be friends. She understands me and she changes. Now she helps me with my English. My friend is black and last year the black people fight with the white people at school and it was terrible. Everyone is running and crying and I don't know where to go. The police come with the gas and my face is all red and burning and I think I can't breathe and am going to die. The students and the police all look very angry and I'm scared of everyone. I see the students say many, many bad words to the teacher and I don't like that. My mother worries that the black people are bad because of the things she sees on the TV, but I will have a friend of any color if they are a good person. I have one friend that is Chinese and some people say bad things to him because he cannot understand, so I say, "I don't want you to treat him like that," because I remember what it felt like.

One of my favorite things about this country is that there are so many different kinds of people. In Mexico, you only see the Spanish-speaking people. I'm a funny Mexican, because I like more when it's cold than when it's hot. The first time we see snow, my mother thought rice was falling from the sky. That would be nice, but I like the snow, too! The first thing I notice when I get here is how tall are all the people. I always have to look way up at the face. I like that they are so big.

Going to school is more better for me than just staying at home, where there is always such work to do. Even when I am very sick with the temperature, I go to the school. I never miss. It's more quick to walk than to take the bus, but I don't mind the walking. We have no word for "teenager" in Mexico. I don't know what that is. I could not go to school in Mexico. There are no jobs either. The life is much more hard. Here I feel like if you make up your mind to do something, you can go and do it. When I graduate from the school, I would like to be a chef. I think I could be a good one!

Lindsay Matson

age 18

"School is funny. You either 'get it' and you can practically sleep walk through the whole routine, or you 'don't get it' and it's a stress-filled struggle."

I just graduated from high school, and I must say I'm glad to have that experience behind me. I never got too involved in any team spirit. I've always hated team sports — simply despise them. I made good grades without trying very hard, even taking advanced courses like calculus and fifth-year Latin. I applied to one college early admission and got in, so I sort of skipped most of that senior year anxiety. I'm really looking forward to going off to school next year, being away from home and more on my own. My home life has been unusual in its usualness — a mom and dad, a brother, and a dog. It's kinda like I'm still waiting for the exciting part of my life to begin.

The day I turned eighteen, I got my eyebrow pierced. I always thought it looked cool and it felt like an act of independence to get it done. My older brother is extremely conservative, so my parents haven't had a lot of experience with teenage rebelliousness. Even though they don't like the way it looks, I don't think they even notice it any more. I've been a vegetarian for quite a while now and they're supportive of my diet. The rest of the world is not as supportive since I pierced my eyebrow. Storekeepers look at me like I might steal something. I couldn't get a summer job because of it. I got hired at a pizza parlor, then was fired when I wouldn't take it out. I tried to explain that it would close up without a retainer, which I didn't have with me, but I was sent home. Even Hardee's, which is always desperate to find workers, wouldn't hire me.

Employers treat kids like crap. I finally found a job at a florist, but the owner kept accusing me of all these things I didn't do, so I finally quit in frustration. Being young sometimes makes you feel like a second-class citizen. I hope when people my age become owners and managers one day, we'll remember what it felt like to be treated with such disrespect and will behave better ourselves. It seems like so many adults always expect the worst from kids, like we're all in gangs or on drugs. It makes everyone feel like it's a "them" and "us" situation. Grown-ups should remember the cliché they teach their kids — "you can't judge a book by its cover." They should get to know someone before they form an opinion of their character.

My teachers always treated me pretty well, even though they always said I wasn't pushing myself to my fullest potential, which was true! School is funny. You either "get it" and you can practically sleep walk through the whole routine, or you "don't get it" and it's a stress-filled struggle.

Patrick McQuilkin

age 15

"School is a totally different experience than skating. The opposite, really. Sitting cooped-up inside, trying to hold still and listen to all this boring stuff that you're not interested in is not my first choice of how I'd like to spend my day. It's almost like time moves at a slower speed in the classroom."

To this day, I still look up to my older brother a lot. He always did a lot of surfing and skating and I was right there behind him, watching his every move. We built a skate ramp in the back yard a couple of years ago. It even has lights, so we can keep going after dark. I'd much rather go out and skate than sit around and watch TV. I've always liked to keep moving and stay busy, whether it's riding a bike or building a tree fort when I was little, or surfing and skating now. Even though I love both, for me skating is the most fun of all. It seems like everyday you can learn something new. I feel like I can be more creative on a skateboard than a surfboard. For some people, it's the other way around. My little brother is probably a better surfer than skater, but like me, he loves both.

Now school is a totally different experience than skating. The opposite, really. Sitting cooped-up inside, trying to hold still and listen to all this boring stuff that you're not interested in is not my first choice of how I'd like to spend my day. It's almost like time moves at a slower speed in the classroom. It seems like sometimes the clock just won't move, especially on a pretty day. Homework is also a pain. Some kids are really into school, but Lord knows why. My parents are always telling me how I have to settle down and get prepared for the "real world," but school doesn't seem very realistic to me.

I've lived in the same house out in the country all my life and we've fixed it up really cool, really made it our own, not only with the ramp, but with hand-painted tiles and things like that. Most of my friends live in neighborhoods, where there's nothing much to do but hang out at someone's house. Going to the mall isn't all that exciting to me either. It seems like a waste of time. They love coming to my house, because we can rage around outdoors without any neighbors to bother. If we want to use the skate ramp at midnight, no one complains. There's probably not a day that goes by when I don't get on my board. Sometimes at night, eight or nine kids will come over to the ramp and that's a lot of fun. My girlfriend surfs a little bit, but very few girls skate, especially on the ramps. It seems to be mainly a guy thing. Girls are more afraid of getting hurt. Sometimes I think she resents how much time I spend on the ramp. Like most girls, she's more serious about things. It's almost like girls seem more grown-up. I'm not much of a worrier or a planner. I tend to live in the moment.

I really love being a kid. I'm in no particular hurry to be a grown-up. I don't even have my learner's permit, even though I've been old enough for almost a year, I haven't got around to it. I love to go back deep in the woods and go camping. Cook up a big ole fat breakfast in the morning. It's always an adventure. I love to go marsh tromping. We wade out into the muck and get caked in mud. The dogs come along with us and have as much fun as we do. You can spend all day out there and have no worries.

Oh Joon Moon

age 18

"In Korea, if you don't do the homework, the teachers hit you. Here the teachers just embarrass you in front of the whole class. For a boy like me, that is much worse than being hit."

I grew up in Seoul, Korea — pretty much an average Korean kid, who, like all my other friends, was fascinated by the United States. When I was sixteen, my parents gave me the opportunity to go to another part of the world to get a wider point of view, and my first choice was America. I used to like the American programs on TV, like *Jeopardy*, because I was studying English in school and it helped me be especially good at it. That was one of my best subjects, even before I had plans to go to America. Of course, since I was about thirteen, I wanted to come here. The music, the styles, the movies that everyone likes in Korea, are all American. I like to wear the baggy clothes and listen to rap music, but it's not like I'm a gangbanger or anything — I just like that style of clothes and music. Puff Daddy, Cyprus Hill — groups like that are banned in Korea because of the lyrics, which is kind of funny because no one can understand what they're saying anyway! When I go back for a visit in Korea, all my old friends want me to bring them clothes and music from the United States.

The education system is so much harder in Korea, especially if you want to go to college. It's just study, study, study all the time. I just hated that system — I felt like I was compressed in a box. When I first came to this country, I was surprised that all the students my age had been playing sports since they were little kids. I do weightlifting right now, and this winter I'm going to wrestle. In the spring, I'll be on the tennis team. I'm actually much bigger physically now than I probably would be if I had never left Korea. I certainly wouldn't be playing all these sports over there. American kids are so physically active and I think that shows part of America's strength as a world power — not only in economic dominance, but the fact that the kids are actually physically stronger because of all the sports they play.

Being in the United States has been an amazing opportunity to meet so many different types of people. Remember, in Korea, everyone's much more alike. The one thing that I can't get used to here is how it seems like as soon as you make friends, they move away. You have to learn to make friends quickly and then let go of them quickly when they move on. People come, people go, all the time in America. It's so wide, there's so much space here, people can get really far away from each other. I have a sense of having more space around me. It is not so crowded as it is at home.

I love the sense of freedom I have here. It's hard to explain the tremendous pressure the Korean academic system puts on you. It's depressing, like you're being pressed into a small square. Here, you have more choices of what to study, and everyone just takes for granted that they do other activities outside of the classroom. In Korea, if you don't do the homework, the teachers hit you. Here the teachers just embarrass you in front of the whole class. For a boy like me, that is much worse than being hit. I'm used to having a great distance between me and the teacher, but here the students and teachers talk to each other with no distance. For Americans, it might make them feel more comfortable, but for me, it doesn't seem respectful. In Korea, if someone is even just a few years older, you treat them with more respect, but here the kids talk to the adults just like they do with each other. I'm used to it now, but my parents can see the change in my manners with them when I come home, and they don't like it.

After I graduate from college, maybe somewhere in Boston, I'll probably go back and work for my father's lighting company. That's one of the reasons he wanted me to go to school in this country. He needs someone in his business who can speak English fluently, so he can start to do business with American companies. It seems like everyone wants to be involved with America.

Cam Powell

age 16

"I think I can get along with adults much better than most kids my age, because I'm not so isolated from grown-ups as kids who are sitting together in school all day. High school is a kind of teenage ghetto. I'm fortunate to have friends of all different ages because of my surfing."

I just had my sixteenth birthday last week. I got my own surfboard at nine and used my older friends' boards before that. I had a friend whose dad was a surfer and he'd take us with him all the time. By the time I turned ten, I was competing in contests. I placed pretty well right away, so after just a few contests, I got sponsored by a local surfboard company and started competing regularly, usually getting firsts, so I decided to go on to bigger contests and started traveling up and down the east coast, competing from New York to Florida.

This summer I was in five contests in California. Rusty surfboards and clothing and Oakley sunglasses, along with 17th Street Surf Shop, help me with my traveling expenses and entry fees. I made my first surf trip to Costa Rica with my brother when I was thirteen and loved the great waves in a tropical environment. I went back in February with a couple of friends and we traveled all over both coasts this time. If I wasn't doing home school, I'd be starting my sophomore year. Some school in Nebraska develops my curriculum. They send me all my books, schedules and deadlines and even send people to my house from time to time to make sure I'm learning. There's a professional surfer on the circuit who oversees my tests, but otherwise it's pretty much up to me to get my work done.

I think I can get along with adults much better than most kids my age, because I'm not so isolated from grown-ups as kids who are sitting together in school all day. Highschool is kind of a teenage ghetto. I'm fortunate to have friends of all different ages because of my surfing.

For me, surfing is not just a sport, it's a whole way of life. I definitely wouldn't be who I am if I didn't surf. It's the number one thing in my life. In big waves, like we had in Mexico, your heart gets pumping, not from paddling, but because you fear for your life. A thirty foot wave is pretty humbling. You can't wear a leash in waves that size, because if you fall, the waves are so powerful, they'll rip your leg off. You've got to be in terrific shape to surf competitively or in big waves. Me and my friends don't ever smoke cigarettes or pot and only rarely drink — never before a contest. I definitely have a healthier lifestyle because of my love for the sport. Most of us eat healthy food and work out for that competitive edge. Sure there's the surfers that lead a real degenerate lifestyle, but they get left behind, and that's not where I want to be. I'm not sure, really, why surfers have such a bad reputation. I mean, most of us are not reeling around stoned going "What's up, dude?" I don't know one single person like that. I think our relationship with the beach and the ocean makes us more concerned about the environment than the average kid.

Pretty much wherever you pollute, it's going to go into the ocean. If you throw trash on the street, it ends up in the storm drain and eventually makes its way to the sea. I don't even spit gum on the ground, because I hate stepping in it. If there's any trash on the beach, I pick it up. It's a surfer thing to leave the beach cleaner than it was when we got there. I got a fungus on my face from surfing in dirty water in California. It's gross. We've got to protect our oceans. It's insane that the storm drains flow untreated into our oceans or that cities haul their garbage out to sea.

Keith Anderson

age 18

"The biggest problem in public school right now is that the kids want to appear cool by acting like they know it all and that makes them afraid of making an effort in class, because they don't want to make a mistake. That was the biggest difference to me when I went to private school. The kids there wouldn't be ashamed to ask questions when they didn't understand something."

In the District's public schools, it's just terrible. My old school district, the H. D. Woodson High School, is in the middle of about five different ghettos, and all of these neighborhoods don't like each other, so it's a bit like a war zone. Fights will break out over nothing. You can accidentally step on someone's foot and your life will be on the line. It's crazy. Everyone's worried about getting disrespected instead of thinking about respecting others. Fortunately for me, my parents didn't raise me that way. It seems like a lot of kids I went to junior high with were hardly raised at all.

I started playing police league football from the time I was eight until the eighth grade. A recruiter from a private prep school, looking for minority students, showed us a video of the place, and I'd never seen such a beautiful place. I brought an application home and at first my mother didn't like the idea. She felt like she wasn't being a good parent to send me off. I think a lot of her friends thought I must have gotten in trouble or something because it is pretty unusual for anyone from our neighborhood to go off to boarding school. They probably thought I was sent off to reform school! I know my parents are glad now that they let me go. There's no doubt that I've gotten a much better education than I ever could have gotten at the local high school. I had to repeat the ninth grade in order to go, and it was still plenty hard work. It was quite a culture shock. I never had a white student in a class with me until I went to boarding school and then I was the only black student in the class, but I think all teenagers are pretty much alike. They have the same feelings for their friends and family.

The biggest problem in public school right now is that the kids want to appear cool by acting like they know it all and that makes them afraid of making an effort in class, because they don't want to make a mistake. The kids come to class with this mask on, trying to appear hard, and they can never take it off and open themselves to learning. That was the biggest difference to me when I went to private school. The kids there wouldn't be ashamed to ask questions when they didn't understand something. It was amazing to me how the teachers always made themselves available to the kids to give them extra help if they needed it. It took me a while to figure out that it was O.K. to get extra help. The teachers at prep school can afford to care about their students because most of us will probably do all right for ourselves. In my old public school, the teachers avoid getting too involved with the students, because too many of them die. One of the teachers at Woodson has been there for seventeen years and seen over two hundred kids murdered. Three of my friends from there were killed in just a few weeks last year. I've been away at school for three years now and I sometimes forget to watch my back when I'm back in the District. Last spring break a guy put a gun to my head for twenty dollars. That probably wouldn't have happened if I hadn't dropped my guard, but after life on dorm, I get used to feeling safe, and of course that makes me be in more danger when I'm back on the streets at home.

One of the best things my college prep school has taught me is that just loafing around, going with the flow and being mellow might get you by while you're living with your parents and going to an easy high school, but life won't be so pleasant once you're grown and on your own if you haven't learned how to be organized and responsible. I really don't have any fantasies of being rich or famous. I just want to be comfortable — be able to take care of my family without worrying about money all the time. By getting the education that's preparing me for college, I think I've got a good chance of achieving my goal.

George Powell

age 17

"As soon as I turned sixteen, I started working for my dad full time. School was so boring, and now I'm never bored. I never felt I had much use for Algebra or Latin, but now I'm learning stuff every day that I'll be able to use for the rest of my life."

My dad started a masonry company forty-five years ago. Business boomed right away, and since then he's made and lost a lot of money. That's the thing about the building business. It's boom or bust. I've been working for him since I was fifteen. I never really accelerated academically in school and was always a lot more interested in working with my dad than going to class or doing my homework. I know I've got a lot of common sense. I'm far from stupid, but I just can't stand sitting in class. As soon as I turned sixteen, I started working for my dad full time. Neither one of my parents had gone to college, so it wasn't a big deal to them that I wanted to work instead of go to school. I figured the stuff I needed to learn was on the job instead of in the classroom. Right now I could go anywhere and earn eighteen dollars an hour as a mason, but I plan on running my own business in the future. My dad is teaching me everything he knows. He's showing me how to make estimates and talk with clients on the telephone. Working together has definitely made us closer. I'm the only one out of four kids that is this dedicated to the business. I love it. I wouldn't do anything differently.

My job in the company right now is to go to each job site and make sure that the work is up to our standards and that our equipment is cared for. I do everything from picking up trash, to figuring out plans, laying block, and driving the forklifts and dump trucks. I'm pretty good with diesel engines and often do mechanical repairs. I'm definitely not afraid of getting my hands dirty. Last winter, when we were really busy, I worked seven days a week, for ten hours a day, for six weeks straight. Two days ago I had to get up at 4:30 in the morning to get the forklift running before the crew started work at seven. I pretty much have to cover everyone else's mistakes and that can be pretty stressful. Today I had to go over to a job and fix a broken masonry saw and the other one broke down while I was still fixing the first one. After I fixed the second one, they broke the mortar mixer. While I'm fixing that, they let the fork lift run out of diesel fuel. After I prime that and get it running again I say, "If anything else breaks, you're paying for it."

Most of the laborers are a lot older than me, but I know who to listen to and who has to answer to me. It's the superintendents for the general contractors that really have a problem with my age. I've pulled my guys off the job if I don't think the general contractors have the site ready for my crew, and some grown-ups have a real problem with a seventeen-year-old shutting them down. Now I get a lot of respect from the guys in our company because they know I'm always looking out for them. They know I know most of them have more building experience than I do. Some of them have been with the company since long before I was even born. My job is to make sure the superintendents treat them fair.

I never feel sorry for myself, working so hard. I like being busy solving problems. School was so boring, and now I'm never bored. I never felt I had much use for Algebra or Latin, but now I'm learning stuff every day that I'll be able to use for the rest of my life. I must be a natural born mason, because geometry was something that made sense to me, that I could imagine using outside of the classroom.

After working all summer, I'd sit in class and look at my watch and think, "I'm not making any money." I like making money and I like spending it. I like having money in my pocket to go out to a restaurant or buy myself whatever I need. I know a lot of people think that if you drop out of high school, you're a loser — a slacker. But I love my work and am building a lifelong career for myself. I have a lot of responsibility and that really gets my attention. One of the things I've learned is I can't make excuses. I do my best and take responsibility for my decisions.

POWELL
Masonry
PETTIBONE
0 20 40 60
HOOVER FORKLIFT SALES
PETTIBONE
WARNING
NO RIDING
CAUTION

Jason Bennett

age 17

"It's frustrating to feel like you know things that you can't express. Like Hamlet, it's hard to 'act as swiftly as thoughts of meditation.' We often have insight but lack the ability to act upon it."

People my age question everything and it makes us skeptical, if not cynical. I don't think we're as optimistic as the original hippies, because we see that even after all the social reforms from twenty-five and thirty years ago, the world is still filled with injustice. We have a different kind of ignorance than a generation or two ago. Instead of accepting homophobia, sexism, or racism as God-given rights, we're often unthinkingly accepting of everything. For example, there's a lot of kids in my school who are vegetarian, but couldn't really tell you why. I suppose it's a lot less harmful than being ignorant of why you're being mean to people. I really enjoy my philosophy class because our teacher reminds us that we have to examine what we think as well as what we feel. Teenagers often confuse feeling with thinking. You need to think your way through life and not just blindly feel your way through. It's a right of passage as a teenager to get swept up in your feelings, getting either insanely excited or depressed. The normal teenage depression is really a bit self-indulgent.

I'm starting to recognize that my feelings, that I think are so deep and so meaningful, are just silly little stuff that is written about in Judy Blume books. I can snap myself out of my self-indulgent feelings and start to think. I know kids who have sex or get drunk because they feel like it and they're not really thinking about the consequences. Not that adults don't often react without thinking. You should see them go to the other side of the street when they see one of my Goth friends.

Being a teenager is confusing because our feelings seem so important, yet they're so impossible to communicate. We're young, so we haven't had enough experience expressing ourselves, plus we're trying to establish our identity. It's frustrating to feel like you know things that you can't express. Like Hamlet, it's hard to "act as swiftly as thoughts of meditation." We often have insight but lack the ability to act upon it. Sometimes I think grown-ups assume we don't have complex emotions because we're young, but our reality is very real to us. We tend to be more comfortable in groups than mano a mano. I guess it's easier to hide out in a crowd while you're still figuring things out.

Most high school kids aren't even comfortable on a traditional date — the kind where the guy picks up the girl, meets the parents, and the two spend the evening alone. It's almost like we're scared of too much closeness. I love the idea of exploring yourself by being really close to someone else, and I feel like at any age that's a really healthy thing. A lot of people think that teenagers aren't mature enough to have a "real relationship." It's such a teen taboo to say you're in love, but real love can exist at any age. Marrying your high school sweetheart is pretty weird these days, because, after all, we don't feel like we have to get married to have sex. That doesn't mean that we don't have morals or can't be shocked. If someone has sex with three different people in one week, in almost any group, they'd be considered promiscuous.

When adults tell us that premarital sex or illegal drugs are "bad," that just makes us want to know why for ourselves. Trying to make us afraid doesn't make us "just say no," it makes us curious. When we're told we're "not mature enough" it just makes us want to be. My parents must have done something right, because I'm basically a decent human being. Your mom and dad are your closest role models and I feel sorry for kids that don't like their parents because it would make it pretty hard to feel good about yourself. Laying down the law or ignoring them isn't good enough. Parents have to really pay attention and listen to their kids if they themselves want to be heard.

Anna Grauso

age 17

"The future really scares me. I've always felt this responsibility to know what I want to do with my life. But the truth is, I don't know what I want to do. That's the scariest part of being a teenager – trying to figure out what you want to be when you grow up."

I've always had a fascination with John and Jackie Kennedy. The fifties and sixties seem like a time of hope and ideals. When I moved here from Europe I started to collect all this bright plastic stuff from that era.

My dad is Italian and my mom's from Germany. We lived in Italy for six years until suddenly everything changed. My little brother, who was only a year younger than me, died, my parents got divorced, and my mom and I moved to the United States. I didn't speak English and everything seemed strange and confusing. I've had a hard time with my school work ever since.

I had a terrible head injury the summer before ninth grade. The boom on our sailboat knocked me out and into the water. Everyone says it was a miracle that I didn't drown or die from the scull fracture and brain hemorrhage. I had a really hard time accepting that I was supposed to live and now I struggle with this idea that I'm supposed to do something great with my life because I tricked death. Ever since my brother died years ago, I felt guilty that it wasn't me. When we first moved to this country, I felt so incredibly lonely I'd bury my face in my little brother's clothes and weep. I think the accident brought all those feelings back to me. I started feeling horribly lonely again. My mom and brother were so close that I didn't feel like I could ever make up that loss for her. I think I reminded my dad so much of my brother that I felt like he kept me at a distance. My stepmother doesn't want me to speak my brother's name in front of my dad. When that boom hit me on the head, I thought it was a sign that I was supposed to go and be with my brother.

Even though I live in this house in the backyard all by myself, Mom's over here all the time. It's like she's giving me the things she always wanted when she was my age. When she wanted to buy this really huge house, I didn't like it because she travels a lot and I didn't want to be in that big house all by myself. So she said, "O.K. — you can have a little house of your own." I thought it would be the best thing in the world but sometimes it's kinda lonely. Sometimes what you want doesn't turn out to be all you wanted. My mom and I decorated this place together and she really enjoyed helping me fix the place up — probably more than I did. It seems like I don't have any attachment to this stuff at all — probably because I have everything I want.

The future really scares me. I've always felt this responsibility to know what I want to do with my life. But the truth is, I don't know what I want to do. That's the scariest part of being a teenager — trying to figure out what you want to be when you grow up. Since I've never been a very good student, I'm not sure if I should go to college; yet there's so much to learn, so much to know. I love my dreams more than my schoolwork. Dreams aren't about wanting things, they're about experience. The scary part of real life is making choices. I always worry about what I choose not to do. One thing I do know is I want to be a mother myself one day.

Sara Jane Ashley

age 16

"Where I go to college will probably have a big influence on where I live later on. It seems like a huge decision to make right now – almost like I'd be choosing my destiny."

Sometimes I don't think I fit in Manhattan, at least not in the materialistic, competitive part. Everyone judges each other on what they wear and where they live and I don't really like that. Unlike a lot of New Yorkers, I can imagine living somewhere else. At the same time I'm very attached to Manhattan. Whenever I've been away and I look at that skyline when we're coming back into the city, I tear right up. Just riding down Lexington Avenue in a taxi or walking up Madison Avenue are things I never get tired of — there's so much to look at. I love opening the window at night and letting the sounds and the smell of the city float over me as I fall asleep.

I'm so lucky, because my grandmother takes me to the opera. That's our special time together, and I really love it. She'll buy me opera CDs and I listen to them quite a bit, though mostly I listen to classic rock and roll, bands like Jethro Tull and The Dead. I like just about all music besides heavy metal and country. A lot of popular music right now just seems really trendy. I mean, I don't think my kids will listen to The Spice Girls or Hanson like I do Nina Simone or Otis Redding. I just don't think their music will last.

Now a Phish concert, that's an experience I wouldn't want to miss. It's better than fun. It's as much about being there as listening to the music. There's this wonderful sense of unity in the crowd. Afterwards, kids tend to fragment back into their own separate groups. Even in my small private school, there are separate cliques. I tend to float from group to group at school, but on the weekends, since I don't really "belong" to any one set, my phone probably doesn't ring as much as some other kid's. During the school year, I have to get up by 6:45 every morning, and when there's play practice, I don't get home until 6:30. I'm starving hungry by then, so by the time I finish dinner, it's after 7:00 and I have tons of homework to do. I have absolutely no time for hanging out on the week days. My entire day is scheduled.

If you look at my address book, so many of my friends have different phone numbers, for their mom's place and for their dad's place. Divorce is so common nowadays. Even if one day I marry a rich man, I still want to make my own money and not be financially dependent on my husband. I don't think of a job as just a paycheck. I want it to be a part of my life that excites me.

I really wish my dad's mother, Laura Ashley, was alive. I want to pursue a career in fashion design and she could have taught me so much. I'm sure I have some of her in me, even though she died when I was really little. Most of my friends don't even realize the connection. It's not something I ever talk about because I wouldn't want anyone to think I was bragging, but I'm certainly not ashamed of the fact. If anything, I'm proud that she was my grandmother. I've been sketching clothes for as long as I can remember, but lately I've been experimenting with just pure design. I've been studying French all through school, and one day I'd like to go to design school in Paris. Where I go to college will probably have a big influence on where I live later on. It seems like a huge decision to make right now — almost like I'd be choosing my destiny.

BAZAAR

Ricky Lilly

age 19

"Having earned my own way through academics and sports, I probably appreciate the opportunity to get a college degree more than some kid who just has Daddy write a check. Every dollar that my parents contribute to my education is a sacrifice for them and I'm not going to waste their hard-earned money."

I've always done pretty good in school and have thought about going to college ever since middle school, even though neither one of my parents did. My dad's a boiler operator and my mom does home-care for old and sick people. They're glad to see me go on to college, but if I didn't want to, I don't think they would have put any pressure on me to continue my education. I know they're proud of me, even if the goal is mine more than theirs. They've always been pretty lenient about letting me make my own decisions. I think if your parents give you a lot of freedom and you don't screw up, it gives you self-confidence. And if you do mess up, then your parents can step in and say you're not mature enough for such and such responsibility. The way that parents get their kids' respect is by giving their kids respect and by not being hypocritical, which if you think about it, is sort of disrespectful.

Fortunately for me, my mom and dad have never been particularly church-going. I mean, not only did I always work on Sundays, but it seems like my friends who have really religious parents always have to sneak around, and can never really talk to their parents about how things really are for them. I know my parents have worked really hard for everything they've got and I have a lot of respect for the hard times they've been through. They don't pretend to be perfect and that makes me feel like I could always talk to them about anything.

I've seen both my parents work hard all my life and it seems there's more job security and satisfaction when you have a college education. Things seemed to always be kinda hard on my mom and dad. They work one job here and stay there for a while, then get laid off and have to move and it's not easy to pick up where you left off. If you start over, you have to start all over from the bottom, which can be pretty frustrating. I know they sometimes wish they could have saved more for my college tuition, but having earned my own way through academics and sports, I probably appreciate the opportunity to get a college degree more than some kid who just has Daddy write a check. Once I get there next year, I'm a lot less likely to skip classes or be hung-over when I do show up, because I lose my scholarship if my grades drop. Every dollar that my parents contribute to my education is a sacrifice for them, and I'm not going to waste their hard-earned money.

I've always played sports at school, not because I have any fantasy about being a professional athlete, but because I enjoy it and it's something I'm fairly good at. I'd much rather play football than change tires, and going to class always seemed at least as fun as working in my grandfather's service station. Schoolwork, like sports, is something that I enjoy and can do well in. Even with AP classes, I've got a 3.5 GPA. I've got a good academic scholarship to college, and I plan on playing football as well as track.

I really like the idea of getting a chance to play a few more years of football. I injured my knee at the National Classic track meet and it slowed down my football game more than my pole vaulting. So many of my friends were superior athletes in track, but for one reason or another they weren't able to get very far along in school. Which is a shame, because you can't support yourself or a family as a pole vaulter. Actually, the kids I have the most respect for are the ones who slug away at school, even if academics don't come easy to them. Especially the guys who are the big athletes, because of the whole testosterone thing. I mean a guy's pride is a lot to overcome. I think a lot of guys drop out of school because they're just plain embarrassed that they're so far behind and their image of being cool or hard is much more important to them at that moment.

EXXON
RICKY

The Courage to Heal
the Relaxation Response
MARSHA SINETAR
DEVELOPING A 21ST CENTURY MIND
NO MORE SLEEPLESS NIGHTS
The Broken Mirror
BRAIN LOCK
A Mood Apart
THE QUEST FOR PERSONAL POWER
out of the shadows
Dover Books $1.00-2.00 EACH!
SLEEPING BEAUTY AND OTHER FAIRY TALES
THE BOOK OF PSALMS
VINTAGE BOOKS
POEMS

Kate Erb

age 17

"The soul projects itself through eyes, I'm told, but mine springs out in piles of crazy hair, of spirals colored rust and brown and gold – my mind and mane an unruly pair."

My mom was my piano teacher from kindergarten through high school. I always enjoyed it except for a rough patch at thirteen. Of course, I don't think many thirteen-year-olds enjoy much of anything! I skipped seventh grade, which helped, because at least it got me through the horror of middle school faster, when you're too old to be a child, and too young to be a "real" teenager. In eighth grade I started playing duets with my mom. It wasn't big money, but we played professionally while I was in high school. The discipline that's necessary to study the piano has been helpful in my other interests, like poetry. I'm a natural procrastinator, anyway, so I really need a structure. Somehow, I just graduated Valedictorian, even though I feel like I slack off all the time. For my college entrance essay, I wrote a poem instead of a biographical essay. I still don't like the third quatrain, but I guess I'm not enough of a perfectionist to do anything about it.

I've been working on and off at my grandmother's bookstore for a while now, although my grandmother prefers to have my younger sister there because I am always getting distracted. I can't help but pick up and start skimming the books that I'm supposed to be arranging on the shelves. I've been reading the diaries of Anais Nin, and I could really identify with her being a sort of scared and introverted person, while at the same time seeming rather unconventional. I would really like to be more discrete, but I'm afraid I'm like my mom and have a tendency to just blurt out the first thing that comes into my head. Both of my parents have been really attentive to my sisters and me and even though it's fun to fantasize about being a great writer one day, I think the most important thing I can do is raise my future children well. I look forward to the challenge some day. The best thing my parents did for me was to always encourage me to ask questions. It takes grace to be able to be a good parent. You need to be able to forgive and accept again. When your child makes mistakes, which of course they will, you need to be able to take their hand and say, "I believe in you," and really mean it.

Fiery Spirit

The soul projects itself through eyes, I'm told,
but mine springs out in piles of crazy hair,
of spirals colored rust and brown and gold—
my mind and mane an unruly pair.
They are not ladylike, and brush the edge
of etiquette — rebellious strands that pop
from braids and buns to raise a wispy hedge
like weeds sprung from an ancient statue's top,
and small green questions that would break in time
the stone of dogma's temple down to leas
where mums and pansies thrive on crumbled lime
and redheads charm the honey out of bees.
So let the matrons point and gasp behind.
I will comb my curls and speak my mind.

Cullen West

age 16

"If we pierce our body or make graffiti art, it's not to offend others but to express ourselves. If a kid grows his hair long and then shaves his head, he's just experimenting with his own personal style. It's fun to paint your face, wear weird clothes or do something crazy with your hair. It's just a form of personal expression, a confirmation that you exist."

It seems like even though I'm always thinking, worrying almost, about the future, I say things before I've had time to think about how I'll sound. I get in trouble at school for saying whatever pops into my head. Teachers get mad at me because they think I'm making fun of them. I catch them in a mistake and it really gets on their nerves. When they're not exactly right, I'll make sure I call them on it. I know I should keep quiet, but it's irresistible. Even though I get good grades, my comments on my report card say I have an attitude problem. I seem to have a problem with authority. I guess I've always been annoying to my teachers since kindergarten. The thing is, I enjoy learning — maybe even more than you're supposed to in a classroom situation. I'm not lazy, but I don't like to waste my time. I love learning, but I hate busywork.

I've never felt like I wanted or needed a lot of attention from my parents. I usually like to spend time here, alone in my room. I can go for a week or so without seeing my dad. This summer he's been annoyed that he doesn't see more of me but he goes to work before I wake up and he's in bed when I get home at night. He works twelve hours a day and travels on weekends. My mom usually takes my little brother out with her, so I have the place to myself. I really love my bedroom, up here away from it all.

Listening to music and playing bass is the best part of my life. The music I'm attracted to and the songs I write are dark and depressing, but they don't make me feel sad. When I write about suicide, I don't beautify death. I see it as a horrible place, where the trees are all wilted and the sky rains blood. Ever since I was a little kid, I've been obsessed with the subject (death) — maybe because it's the one sure thing. It's so mysterious, so huge. When I learned that one day the sun would burn out, the thought of cosmic annihilation was overwhelming. I used to have dreams about the earth ripping apart and being sucked into the black hole where the sun used to be. My teachers don't like me writing about death in my schoolwork, but it is hard to ignore. It's not like I have a death wish or even feel depressed. I'm not even particularly moody. My friends would say I'm pretty easy-going. I have a real sense that life isn't infinite and we shouldn't waste it.

Even though I'm pretty laid back, I'd have to say I'm ambitious. I love the attention we get when my band plays before an audience. People yell our names and experience the music. It's great to have the microphone and be up on stage — I wish it would never end.

I just kinda live in my own small circle of friends, so I can't speak for my entire generation — just us. If we pierce our body or make graffiti art, it's not to offend others but to express ourselves. Adults get upset if you don't behave just like them. If a kid grows his hair long and then shaves his head, he's just experimenting with his own personal style. If you find a look that expresses how you feel, it makes you feel good about yourself. It's fun to paint your face, wear weird clothes or do something crazy with your hair. It's just a form of personal expression, a confirmation that you exist.

Tripp Callan

age 18

"I think teenagers can be really judgmental because their own identity is insecure. You're trying to figure out who you are and how you fit in, and if someone is really different than you, you might be a little uncomfortable with that. It's a time in your life when you're looking for a group to identify with — that thing grown-ups call peer pressure."

I think teenagers can be really judgmental because their own identity is insecure. You're trying to figure out who you are and how you fit in, and if someone is really different than you, you might be a little uncomfortable with that. It's a time in your life when you're looking for a group to identify with — that thing grown-ups call peer pressure. I don't think peer pressure is as persuasive as a lot of adults think — at least that hasn't been my experience. For example, the kids that don't smoke or are virgins don't have any outside pressure to behave differently. A majority of the senior class has tried marijuana, but I don't want to do anything to my mind that will make me lose control and no one pressures me to do otherwise. Everyone's an individual, and some people are followers and some are leaders and some are loners.

I've always expected myself to do well in school. I'm not satisfied with anything less than straight As. I work extremely hard, but I enjoy the process and doing a good job makes me happy, so it's not like I'm some drudge. It's something I've always done to and for myself. My parents are always telling me to stop working so hard, but I have to do what I have to do. Mastering the material in school gives me a real sense of accomplishment. The trouble with being in the top of your class is if your GPA is number one, there's nowhere to go but down and that gives you this feeling of constant pressure. Harvard recruited me to play lacrosse and when I went up there and met the coach, I really liked the way the school values both academics and athletics. They have fifteen pre-Meds on the team and that impressed me because I think I want to go into medicine. Everyone there makes good grades and their lacrosse team is in the top ten. It's wonderful to find a place where you really fit in. I was accepted early admittance so I can relax a little bit now. It's a nice relief to know where you're going to college. I'm sure I'll still make good grades because I enjoy the learning process and I like doing well. If you're a perfectionist, anything less than your best is not good enough.

I have confidence in the classroom and on the playing field, but girls are more of a challenge. If I am really attracted to a girl, it's hard for me to tell if she feels the same way. Some guys seem to have the knack, but I'm not too confident in that department. If you like to be in control of the situation and see what's ahead of you, it's a lot easier to do that on a report card or score board than it is in a romantic relationship. Actually it's an area of my school life where I'm probably more like everyone else. I assume I'll get married one day but it's like growing old, I don't think about it. Right now I enjoy the idea of infinite opportunity.

When you're my age, it's kinda hard to believe that you're mortal. That's probably a marker of adulthood, when you realize your possibilities are finite and you are not immortal. Of course I realize death is real, but probably not in the same way as someone whose parents or children have died. Even though I'm the type of person who's always planning and building for the future, I've always admired the kids whose motto is "live for the day." I'm not sure whether they are courageous or reckless, but they sure are different from me. Sometimes I feel guilty because I've had such a good life so far, but I soon realize that if that's the case, I should feel gratitude instead of guilt.

STAB
27
LACROSSE
STAB
LACROSSE
BRINE

Lucy Smith

age 16

"Parents think they know what we're going through, because they were our age once, but the world is a different place in 1997 than 1967. Kids in junior high school are facing decisions that their parents didn't have to make until college."

I went to the same small private school from first grade until Thanksgiving of this year. When you're in such an isolated environment for that long you become insulated from issues that don't effect your little world. I guess parents send their kids there because it is secluded and protected, but I felt myself struggling to move out into a larger world. Even though my old school has great teachers that really care about you, it felt like this really heavy weight after a while. Everyone knows everything about everyone and the school's safety net system started to feel confining. My mom being a teacher there probably contributed to my feeling a lack of privacy. My dad had gone to my school when he was a kid and I think that made me feel guilty that I didn't really like the place. I was always so stressed over homework and sports that it was hard to get out of bed in the morning. I used to always feel like I was trying to catch up academically, like everyone else was a step ahead.

At Saint Anne's almost everyone is a competitive student and athlete. I'd come home from sports so tired, I'd be totally overwhelmed by the amount of homework I'd have to face. One of the main reasons I wanted to transfer to a larger school is to be in a less pressured environment, where I could feel relaxed with myself.

My four best girlfriends left for different schools last year and it felt like a huge hole. That was nothing compared to when my dad died Christmas of that year. After that I didn't know what to do with all the pain. It forced me to discover my inner resources. I dreamed about him all the time right after he died and he helped me dig deep and find inner strengths I didn't know I had. That gave me the courage to go ahead and do what I wanted to do all along, which was go to a larger, less competitive school. I've come to believe that every time something awful happens, it's an incredible opportunity to learn something important. When my best friends left school, it was a message to make new friends. When my father died, I learned I could survive anything and that gave me the courage to make a necessary change. I was really close to him and when he died without warning, I was really mad. I felt robbed and I dealt with the anger by fighting with my sister and my mother, who of course were as sad and confused as I was. I've now come to realize that even though his physical presence is gone, he's always with me, in some ways in a more intimate level than when he was alive because now our relationship transcends judgement on both our parts. I have no doubt that I can communicate with him and still lean on his support. Once I knew he wouldn't be at my Saint Anne's graduation, it was much easier to make the decision to do what I had been thinking about for a while. I was aching to leave. I felt like a hermit crab, whose body had outgrown its shell.

Now that I'm in a large public school, we still have tests and homework, but it's not so intense. Lacrosse season's starting, but instead of being second string, I'm one of the better players on the team. It just feels a lot lighter to be in an atmosphere where there are so many different kinds of people. I've only been at my new high school for a little over two months, but the transition has been incredibly easy. I definitely made the right decision for me, even though it might seem a bit panicked-out to transfer in the middle of a semester. Once I decided to leave Saint Anne's, I was already gone mentally, so the next obvious step was to remove myself physically. The high school is so huge compared to where I've been, it took me a few weeks to learn how to get to my classes, but getting lost in the halls was a small price to pay to gain access to a larger world. I'm actually making good grades, which feels really great. The teachers here don't look over your shoulder all the time, but they're available to give help if you ask for it, which is the kind of environment I wanted.

One thing that is kind of weird, or at least different from my experience at my old school, is guys at the high school tend to view girls, especially new girls, as potential date material. At Saint Anne's there are a lot of close friendships between girls and boys that don't have anything to do with dating. I love having guy friends because they're so plain and simple. It seems like girls always want to analyze everything, which can be interesting, but sometimes it's nice to have a conversation that doesn't mean anything except exactly what you said. If I talk to some guy I don't know at the high school, he might think I'm hitting on him instead of just being friendly.

There seems to be more sexual tension in the halls than at my old school, which was more like a family because people knew each other for so long and shared a lot of the same values. In my health class there's a fourteen-year-old girl with a baby, and you see pregnant girls in the halls all the time. We're studying the cost of child care and there are kids in the class with first-hand experience. I can't comprehend having a baby at this age. These kids are tough and think they can take on the world. Being in public school makes me appreciate all the advantages I had at home and at school. Most of the kids at my private school were richer than my family, but now that I see what a lot of kids go home to, and I'm not talking material possessions, I feel really grateful for the way I was raised. Some kids have to raise themselves. I feel better prepared to deal with the present and plan for the future because of the value system I was raised with.

One thing I can't get used to, and I hope I never do, is how disrespectful some people are at my new school. I was taught to make eye contact when you're having a conversation and not to interrupt when someone is talking. I can't believe the cussing in the classroom. I've seen kids tear up demerit slips and throw them in the teacher's face. At my old school, it would be totally forbidden to put your head down on the desk during class. Here it happens all the time. Teachers are just grateful they're not interrupting.

The girls, especially the black girls, at my new school get in really vicious physical fights. It seems like black kids definitely have the most power at the school. They get the most respect because they know how to be hard, act tough and intimidating. There are cops all around the school and you need a written note to even go to the bathroom, but there's still so much more stuff going on than most adults probably want to imagine. Parents think they know what we're going through, because they were our age once, but the world is a different place in 1997 than 1967. Kids in junior high school are facing decisions that their parents didn't have to make until college. When my mom was sixteen she was completely sheltered from drugs, sex, and violence. She went to an all-girls school with a dress code, so she was never intimidated in the halls by boys with a different set of values about how you should look and behave.

It might seem strange that I would leave an environment that was so nurturing for a much more unsafe and erratic place, but I felt suffocated by the familiarity of my old school and weighed down by the competitive pressure. I'm still in the process of discovering who I am, but I needed a less familiar environment to do that and to relieve myself of some academic anxiety that kept me from enjoying school. I'm much happier now than I have been in years. It's still hard to separate my thoughts from my feelings, but at least I know there is a difference. I'm coming to realize that I do have a lot of choices, and that good choices have good consequences and that bad choices have bad consequences.

Ocean Linning

age 19

"I suspect that a lot of teenage suicide comes from not being able to find the closet door. Gay youths are pretty much forced to live a heterosexual lifestyle. It doesn't convert them, it just makes them feel terrible. Adolescence is a difficult time for everyone, but especially for those of us whose sexual orientations don't match society's expectations."

I had figured out by kindergarten that I was different than most of the other boys. I got crushes on other little boys instead of girls. The neighborhood I grew up in in New York was pretty fast. I lost my virginity with an eleven-year-old girl when I was twelve. I had already picked up that being gay was not something you'd want to be, so I faked it as best I could. It wasn't as if I disliked girls — in fact, I liked them a lot. It's just that I was much more attracted to boys. I remember playing house when we were little kids and wishing I could kiss Ricardo instead of Marcie.

I just came out this year and I can hardly express what a relief it is to let go of some of the thoughts that are always building inside my head. It's as if my life up to now has been a secret meditation. All through high school I had one girlfriend after another. I think I was trying to convince myself that I really was straight. I can relate to girls so well that other guys would get jealous — which is really rather funny, when you think about it. No one was out of the closet in high school and I wasn't about to be the first one. I felt so isolated and alone in my sexuality. I fooled around with a friend once and the next day he claimed he was drunk, that he thought I was a girl. Yeah, right — whatever!

That's a time in your life where you need to find a group where you feel like you belong. It was hard enough because I'm of mixed race. The black kids thought I was too white and the white kids thought I was black. It's hard to find your tribe in high school when you don't have any clear cultural origins — and being gay just made things more difficult for me.

My mom started having her suspicions about my true sexual nature by my early teens, but I always denied it. If homosexuality was accepted, I probably wouldn't have dated girls and I almost certainly wouldn't have lied to my mom about my sexual orientation. Now that I no longer deny my homosexuality, I'm really enjoying my feminine side. I cross my legs and twitch across the floor. My hands are just flapping away while I chat. I'm proud of myself that I came out while still in my teens. Most gay kids my age are still hiding deep in the back of the closet.

In a desperate last-gasp effort to deny my true self, I signed up for the Marines my senior year in high school. I was probably looking for a group that I could call my own. I decided if I was going to try to be manly, I might as well hook-up with the most manly of macho men. It's laughable now, but at the time I was desperate. Boot camp was the first place I ever felt like I belonged. Even at home, I felt like my step-dad liked his own kids better than me. I was washed with a wave of pride that felt like a blessing. I'd never excelled in anything athletic and I discovered that I was one of the fastest runners in my platoon. I also discovered that I couldn't bring myself to join in the platoon's ditty, "Right hand, right knee, left hand, left knee, back straight, mouth shut, kill." I looked at the M-16 in my hands and thought, "What am I doing here?"

There was no way out except to convince them that I was insane. Admitting that I was gay would have done the trick, but at that time I thought I'd carry that secret to my grave. No one loves life any more than I do, yet I was willing to risk a suicide attempt in order to protect my big secret. It seems amazing to me now, but it's not easy to break through a lifetime lie. I cut my wrists with my razor, just enough to get their attention but not enough to bleed to death. I've always cried really easily, which was a source of embarrassment growing up, but now that trait served me well because when they sent me to the psychiatrist, tears streamed uncontrollably down my face and as a result they decided to send me home. So much for my failed attempt to be a military man.

Those group showers were terrifying — I was so afraid that I'd get aroused and the other grunts would beat me up. It was almost as if my eyes had a brain of their own. I mean these were some fit guys and it was a constant struggle not to stare. I made an effort to be extremely masculine, but I couldn't maintain the charade.

Last summer I went to Florida to visit my brother and the best club in town was a gay bar. I'd never been to one before and I was so happy to be surrounded by people just like me. I decided to move somewhere with a large gay community. I took the bus to Seattle. I was ready to acknowledge my homosexuality to myself, but I wasn't quite ready to tell my family and friends. What I didn't realize at the time was once I let my feminine side out, it would just pour out with a vengeance. It was impossible to hide once I accepted it myself. When I arrived on Broadway in Capital Hill, I thought I was seeing things. Guys were walking down the street hand in hand. I thought I'd died and gone to heaven. When I asked a girl on the street where the clubs were, she said I was standing in the heart of the largest gay community in North America and most of the clubs in the area were oriented that way and I said, "So am I." It felt strange and liberating to hear those words come out of my mouth. It's like all the butterflies flew out as soon as I opened the closet door.

There's a big community of kids that live on the street there and they took me in and showed me how to get by on very little. We had to move from one campsite to the next to keep from getting arrested for vagrancy. They showed me the public showers and how to get free food. What I really needed was warmer clothes. I was always freezing. I figured out how to couch-surf as much as possible because it was cold.

My mom sent me a bus ticket home and I had mixed feelings about going home. I knew there was no way I could keep pretending to be someone I'm not — no way I could shut myself back in the closet again. Yet at the same time I knew I'd have to reveal my true nature to my family in order to come to terms with myself. Some of my friends thought I was going through a phase, but I knew I was just admitting the way I'd always felt. My mom's reaction was, "I always knew." I'll never forget the feeling of comfort and relief I had when I realized I no longer had to hide. She understands it's not something I chose, any more than heterosexuals choose to be the way they are. I'm loving being myself, especially with my family and friends. It hasn't been always easy. My step-father has been less than supportive. He's worried I'm going to be a "bad influence" on his sons. What he doesn't realize is I can't "turn them gay" any more than he can "turn me straight." I've lost more than a few friends, too, but I've gotten to know who my real friends are. Girls don't seem to care one way or the other, but my heterosexual male friends are a lot more skittish with the news. At first they're all nervous that I'm going to put the moves on them and when I say "You're not my type," it kinda hurts their feelings.

This year I met a high school boy who I thought was really cute. Right away I felt like we had known each other forever. He was going through the very same things that I went through a few years back and he poured out his whole life story to me. I felt like my understanding could really help him, but I guess I couldn't save him all by myself. He needed family and community support as well. I suspect that a lot of teenage suicide comes from not being able to find the closet door. He called me that night before he killed himself, but I wasn't home. I felt really guilty about his death at first, that I either I gave him too much attention or not enough attention. No one really wants to feel completely alone, to be the outcast. The way society thinks about gays and lesbians makes it pretty hard to feel good about yourself. Gay youths are pretty much forced to live a heterosexual lifestyle. It doesn't convert them, it just makes them feel terrible. You might think it sounds romantic, but it's pretty miserable to be a loner. If you have no gay friends, you can feel really isolated since you can't relate to all the boy/girl stuff that other teenagers are always talking about. Adolescence is a difficult time for everyone, but especially for those of us whose sexual orientations don't match society's expectations.

I dreamed your
step, your warmth
against my side & woke
to see weird grey
stars of terror
wheeling around the pole
of midnight
~marge piercy~

Genny Munn

age 14

"It's hard, because we live in a society that worships thinness, so I still equate skinniness with goodness and fat with badness. Most teenage girls struggle with feeling good about their bodies. My body was changing and my family was falling apart. The one thing I could control is how much food I ate and weight loss became some sort of twisted triumph."

When I was twelve years old I started getting hips and my boyfriend dumped me. I didn't like what I saw when I looked in the mirror. It was almost as if I was trying to turn back the clock. I started making myself throw up after I ate anything, in an attempt to keep my body from growing. My parents were getting divorced and I had started a new school and I felt like the only thing I could control was my food intake. I equated thinness with happiness. Starving myself was a quest for feeling in control. I was so depressed after my mom and dad split up, the doctors put me on this antidepressant that had a side effect of making me not hungry. That made it even easier for me to skip breakfast, then eventually lunch and dinner as well. While I was still twelve, I started smoking cigarettes, to cut my appetite even more. Food was the issue for me. Every day was a struggle to resist the hunger, not give in to my appetite. By the time I was thirteen, I had started to smoke pot and write this dark, depressing poetry which dwelled on suicide. At five feet, seven inches, my weight got down to ninety-nine pounds. My parents hardly knew their little girl, and they were scared — so was I.

I was put in a psychiatric hospital and I felt like I was being punished for being a bad person. I cried myself to sleep every night I was there. The food was so gross in the hospital, that I just stopped eating at all. It got to the point where I'd feel like I'd lost control if I ate even one bite of something. One grape made me feel like I'd pigged out. If I lost a pound, I'd feel triumphant, but if I gained even a few ounces, I'd be thrown into despair. That summer between seventh and eighth grade, I started contemplating my own suicide and even went so far as to write a suicide note. That fall, my school sent me home, saying I needed to get well before I could return.

It was hard for my mom to find a treatment center for me because I was younger than the age limit at most eating disorder clinics. I was abusing laxatives and chain smoking in a desperate attempt to control my weight. Those two weeks that I was out of school before I entered the treatment center in Tulsa were a time of incredible closeness between me and my mom. She could have made me feel a lot more guilty for being such a mess, but she didn't. It was really scary to go off there, for such a long time, so far away from home. My mom had to sign papers for them to have electroshock therapy if I needed it, though I never did. It was hard for her to send me so far away, but we were at a point that we were ready to do whatever it takes to get me well. It was an amazing experience for me to meet other anorexics. We felt so close to each other, because even though we came from many different backgrounds, we all really understood each others' pain. It felt good to be understood. It was the first necessary step to healing.

I call my eating disorder "Ed," and I've learned how not to listen to that craziness and not abuse my body. It's hard, because we live in a society that worships thinness, so I still equate skinniness with goodness and fat with badness. Most teenage girls struggle with feeling good about their bodies. I mean, very few girls are pencil thin with large breasts like the models in the magazines or movie stars. You start to think, "If I looked like them, I wouldn't have any problems." For anorexic girls, it's not a quest for some ideal of beauty as much as a struggle for control. My body was changing and my family was falling apart. The one thing I could control is how much food I ate and weight loss became some sort of twisted triumph. Even though I'm eating now, I'm still not completely at peace with my relationship with food. But when I do eat now, food tastes really wonderful to me, after depriving myself for so long. I expect I'll always be terrified of becoming fat.

Your skin like dawn Mine like
One paints the beginning of a certain
The other
of a sure beginning
baaba seth
angel

Some of my friends from the anorexic clinic still haven't learned that there's so much more to life than a scale. I missed a lot of things last year and I'm grateful to be living at home, going to school and having friends. "Ed" is still in the background noise of my life, but the disease is not my whole life any more. When "Ed" runs your life, you can't have a life outside of your obsession with weight loss. You're too self-absorbed to be a good daughter, sister, or friend. You hate yourself. Few people understand that.

I know I'm young and I don't expect to be treated like an adult, but I would like to be treated like a human being. If grown-ups would be more candid with young people, it wouldn't distress them, it would help them sort things out and have hope for the future. When my teacher tells me about the problems she had when she was growing up, it gives me hope that I can overcome my problems, too.

My mom and I can talk about anything and everything together. Some girls don't even tell their moms when they get their period, which seems really weird to me. All the hell I went through with my eating disorder, my parents went through with me, and although I'd never wanted to cause them any pain, the pain we shared when I was so sick made us unusually close. My mom and I were always close. She was always involved and there for me. By the teen years, it's too late to try and start up a tight relationship with your kid. When my anorexia started taking over at puberty, I doubt my mom would have even had a chance of helping me get well if I didn't already know that I could count on her to be on my side.

Sarah Parnell

age 17

"Marijuana has been used for mind enhancement, for spiritual purposes, for ages. Anything can be abused and misused, but cannabis is not in itself bad. Sex is the same way. It's a responsibility, to be treated with respect, but there's nothing wrong with it."

When I read articles in the news magazines about kids my age, it sounds like we're always up to no good. It seems like teenagers never get any attention unless they're doing something wrong. I certainly don't feel that my generation is as hopeless as the media makes us out to be.

In my high school, there's all different kinds of groups: the jocks, the freaks, the preps, the gangstas. Everyone wants to be an individual and at the same time, part of a group. As far as my own personal style, I've always worn big clothes — maybe because I used to wear my big brothers' clothes. The main thing is, it's comfortable. I can hang out with surfers and skaters as well as punk rockers or rednecks and still feel comfortable about myself. I've pretty much dressed the same way since my mom stopped dressing me in kindergarten. Dresses are just not me — never have been. If you feel comfortable with yourself, then you can hang with all kinds of different people and not get sucked in too deeply. The teen years are the first time you make choices for yourself and get to know yourself by the choices you make. It helps to have an open mind. I try not to identify too strongly with any individual group. Just because I don't wear my hair in a neat little bun, and wear a sweet little dress with a string of pearls, doesn't mean I want to tear down society. I just don't need to please anyone but myself. The way to have self respect is to be who you are comfortable being. If you have respect for yourself, you tend to respect other people.

Look at the way a lot of people judge reggae music. Bob Marley sings about the worth of each individual. When he sings about Jah, he's talking about God, but people who aren't into his music think he's singing about dope. It might be easier to judge than to understand, but that doesn't make it right. Marijuana has been used for mind enhancement, for spiritual purposes, for ages. Anything can be abused and misused, but cannabis, like reggae music, is not in itself bad.

Sex is the same way. It's a responsibility, to be treated with respect, but there's nothing wrong with it. Like drugs, or even food, it can be misused; but to love someone and be loved back is hardly wrong. You can protect yourself from unwanted pregnancy or disease, but your heart is always at risk when it comes to physical attraction. A broken heart is one of the most painful things that can happen to you because there's nothing you can do for it. You can get a cast or stitches when you break or cut your arm, but with a heart you just sit there and hurt.

I'm lucky I have brothers because it's taught me not to expect guys to act like girls — I know they're different. I feel like it's easier to be friends with guys because there's no competition between us like there is with another girl. Guys are definitely competitive between themselves, maybe even more so. Girls are better at being sympathetic, but guys are better at making a plan to fix a problem.

When I grow up I'd really like to be a psychologist because human nature is never boring. I want to experience all that I can and learn about other peoples' experiences because the world is totally different for each person. Everyone has their own unique eyes to see the world. When you share information, you learn other points of view. That's why I love photography, too. You get to share your vision, but of course everyone sees your pictures through their own eyes.

GUESS

Jamila Smith

age 17

"We get *Newsweek* at school and I have to wonder where some of those writers get their ideas. They act like drugs and alcohol are the biggest problems in the whole world. What's important is an individual's attitude towards those things. If they're not a big deal in your life, then they're not a big deal."

Right now in school, they have us reading *The Catcher in the Rye.* J. D. Salinger is a very good writer, but I just didn't care for the book. The character Holden seems kinda self-centered. He is trying to find himself, but to me he seems spoiled and judgmental. A lot of grown-ups think all teenagers are like that, but even though we're trying to figure things out, we aren't so harsh as Holden Caulfield. We're not all unsympathetic and narrow-minded.

Senior year in high school is kinda scary. The whole world is out there like a big question mark. I tell myself to live one day at a time, but then I find myself worrying — college or culinary school? Will I get in? Can I afford it? It's impossible for me to see past two or three years from now. I'm certain I'm destined to do something, I'm just not sure what it is. You see so many adults just walking around all gloomy, like they're hating life. I certainly am going to try my best to stay lighthearted.

We get *Newsweek* at school and I have to wonder where some of those writers get their ideas. They act like drugs and alcohol are the biggest problems in the whole world. What's important is an individual's attitude towards those things. If they're not a big deal in your life, then they're not a big deal. There's usually pot or beer around somewhere, but for most teenagers it's not the most important thing in the world to them. As for cocaine and heroin, I don't think you'll find many kids at all that are interested in messing around with that stuff. No one that I know thinks it's cool to be a drug addict. I don't feel a lot of pressure to smoke weed or get drunk when I'm out with my friends. I'm not saying these things don't happen, I'm just saying things don't seem to me to be so rock-bottom, out of control as *Newsweek* would have you believe. With teenagers, there's a lot more talking than doing. I don't know why the media thinks it can stereotype kids when adults are seen more as individual. It's a bad idea to define any group as all alike. Some kids have sex and some don't. Some drink and smoke and some don't. We're individuals, just like grown-ups.

Things have not changed all that much since our parents were kids, especially the double standard. Girls still have to watch their reputations. If you even hang out with someone at school who they call skank or trashy, it can hurt your own reputation. The same boys who talk so bad about these girls would brag about doing the same things themselves. The news magazines make it sound like teenage girls think it's cool to get a baby. There are quite a few pregnancies in my school, but I don't know anyone who got that way on purpose or was happy to discover they were. Sex can be a good thing or a bad thing, depending on how it's used. It's a natural part of life and I do think it's a good thing that people can talk more openly now than they used to. It's too important a subject to ignore. Parents should talk to their kids about sexual responsibility before they get to junior high. That's not too soon. I think there's more pressure on kids to have sex than there is to smoke and drink. Hormones are there whether we talk about it or not and they are hard to ignore, especially if you don't know what's going on. You can "just say no" but sex isn't going to go away. All it does is stop all conversation. A teenager has to find that point between being self-destructive and being afraid to live.

Your parents can't have a life for you. You've got to make your own mistakes. If we don't always tell our parents everything that is going on with us, it's mostly because we do love them and don't want to face their disapproval. Parents have to remember that their children are not the enemy.

Rebecca Dill

age 17

"As far as sex is concerned, teenagers are full of hormones and curiosity, so it's crazy to try and deny us access to information. The more we know, the more informed decisions we can make. Ignorance and fear just result in unplanned pregnancy or sexually transmitted disease."

My parents have always given their kids' needs a lot of respect, whereas a lot of parents are so busy dispensing rules and advice, they don't really notice what their kids' needs are. Of course, I've never been particularly self-destructive, but sometimes I'm reminded of the expression, "The tighter you hold sand in your hand, the more it slips through your fingers." It often seems like the kids with the strictest parents are the ones that run wild. My freshman year I pierced my navel, just to try it, really — it wasn't a big deal. It was kinda cool, but after the novelty wore off, I took it off and haven't thought about it since. My parents were surprised, because they thought it wasn't like me; but your teenage years are a time to experiment and figure out what you're "really like." I think if there's a lot of mutual respect, like there is in our family, that kids will almost unconsciously take on their parents' values. They raised us in the Unitarian Church, which is very accepting and forgiving. I haven't become sexually active yet, but when I'm ready, I wouldn't hesitate to talk to my parents about birth control, because we weren't taught that sex is shameful. Some adults seem to think that just because you know about birth control, that you're going to go out and have sex! I think it's sad that so many young people learn about sex through this filter of fear and shame. My family and my Church taught me to respect myself and others, but that doesn't mean I expect to stay a virgin until I get married. Both boys and girls need to be taught responsibility, but that doesn't always mean "saying no." Sometimes it's appropriate to say "yes."

The old double standard is very much around. A guy who sleeps around is a real cool "Mack Daddy," but a girl can still be called a slut. It's still more acceptable for a boy to experience sex as a physical release, but a girl is held to a higher standard, like she's supposed to be more spiritual or something.

It seems to me that the more taboo you make a subject, the more obsessed people become. Look at the stupid twenty-one-year-old drinking age. Binge drinking and alcohol abuse are the result. As far as sex is concerned, teenagers are full of hormones and curiosity, so it's crazy to try and deny us access to information. The more we know, the more informed decisions we can make. Ignorance and fear just result in unplanned pregnancy or sexually transmitted disease. I mean, I know what a condom is, but I'm still a virgin because I haven't wanted to be that close to anyone yet.

Another obsession of my generation is weight. I know I'm not overweight as far as my health is concerned, but it seems like it's impossible for me to feel "thin enough." Being super slim is so much in fashion, that when I go to a clothes store with stuff for kids my age, even the largest size is too small. I get in this cycle of exercising and dieting for a few weeks and then just giving up because it's just impossible for me to look like Kate Moss. It's scary to think I used to wish I was bulimic or anorexic, so I could look like my skinny friends. I love good food and I hate to throw up, so I guess I'm stuck with my body type. A lot of girls smoke so they won't gain weight. Now that's really stupid, but it shows this irrational worship of thinness. We're so surrounded by advertising, we forget that most girls aren't thirty pounds underweight and air-brushed! Every time after I go shopping for pants, I loose my friendly relationship with food for a while. And bathing suits — forget it! I won't even try them on. I think I'm a secure and confident person, but my body is the one thing I'm self-conscious about. My best friend has a perfect little body in a string bikini and I won't even wear shorts. The crazy thing is the girls with the fashion-model figures often worry about their weight as much as I do. Teenagers are so critical of both themselves and each other. If only we were back in the Renaissance, when cellulite was attractive; or at least the 1950s, when Marilyn Monroe's chubby upper arms were considered sexy!

Ana Klausmann

age 17

"I think the American culture is really into punishment and promoting fear. It's almost as if the powers-that-be want a girl's life to be destroyed as a punishment for having sex."

I'm not an American citizen, so I can't collect food stamps. That's just as well because I have a lot of disgust with the American government — a lot of rich white men who are close-minded. They've made teenage mothers and immigrants the scapegoats for a lot of the country's problems. I guess it's easier to attack those who can't really defend themselves. I think the American culture is really into punishment and promoting fear. It's almost as if the powers-that-be want a girl's life to be destroyed as a punishment for having sex. A lot of the talk shows about teen pregnancy begin with the question, "When did you realize that your life was ruined?" I think that's a mean-spirited assumption. There's such a big fuss over girls getting abortions, you'd think it was a common form of birth control instead of a difficult life choice. I don't know anyone who hasn't agonized over the decision, no matter what they decide to do. The best decision anyone can make is their own decision, not trying to second guess what other people want. Politicians and parents can't live your life for you.

My pregnancy put a big strain on my relationship with my boyfriend. I felt like I was turning into his mom, telling him what to do, and I didn't like that any more than he did. The changes of pregnancy affect the mother much more than the father, and that pulled us apart instead of together. I've certainly taken a lot better care of myself than I would have if I hadn't gotten pregnant. I never went through any period of regret — "Oh, my youth is over, blah, blah, blah"— but I think my boyfriend has. I think my maternal instincts over-rode such thoughts.

Both of our parents are divorced. I think it's a lot harder to hold a relationship together with a guy than it is to love your child. We might get married one day, but neither one of us is in a big hurry. I'm much more ready to be a mother than a wife. I really like being home with my baby all day. I love the work of child care, but I'm not too happy about being financially dependent. I'm not very trusting of people, so it's scary to rely on someone. In my class at school, only two families out of twenty-two hadn't been divorced. My own dad wasn't very consistent about child support and I only saw him a few weeks a year. I think it'd be really nice for me and my son to have a man to rely on, but it's apparently easier said than done. Once a man cheats on you it's really hard to trust him again and I'm afraid it's really hard for a man to stay faithful.

I'm happy right now to just focus on raising my kid. I don't think a baby really holds you back as much as everything takes more time. You just have to be a little bit more patient to get to do what you want to do. I've already gotten my GED, when most kids my age are still in high school. I guess one good thing about becoming a mother when you're sixteen is that by the time he's in school, I'll just be turning twenty-one. When I do establish a career, it won't be any harder for me than it is for a career woman to adapt to motherhood. I've still got my whole life ahead of me. Just because I'm a mom, it doesn't mean all doors are closed to me forever. Being a mother has really taught me to trust my instincts. I feel a lot more secure now that I'll be able to recognize opportunity when it comes along. Everybody is so different, there's no one right way to make a satisfying life for yourself. Having a healthy, happy baby has given me a huge sense of accomplishment. He's physical proof that I can do something well and I feel like I can do anything if I put my mind to it.

Molly Dewey

age 18

"I think the double standard is unfair and still around. Guys certainly don't have a problem separating sex from love, but somehow girls aren't supposed to experience desire without being 'in love' first."

I grew up in a typical suburban neighborhood, the kind of place where people use Saturdays to wash the dog and mow the grass. My dad's a doctor and my mom's a nurse, so obviously they place a lot of importance on education but, unfortunately, I've never been much of a student. It's like school could never really capture my attention. I skipped classes all the time. When I was there, I was always falling asleep. When I was in boarding school, I smoked a lot of weed, but by the time I was in senior high, I got kinda bored with it. I got sick of being tired all the time. I still smoke cigarettes, which my parents hate, but they're relieved that I'm not stoned all the time. The ironic thing is, if marijuana was legalized it would be much more difficult for kids to get. It's hard for us to buy beer because its sale is closely controlled, but you can buy pot really easily. I used to get a big kick out of tripping at school. It made class a lot less boring. My GPA and SAT scores were so low, I didn't even bother applying to college. I'm enrolled in massage school, which is great, because I'd much rather be a massage therapist than be stuck in some office.

I have a group of friends that mean the world to me. We're incredibly close and whenever we're together, I feel incredibly safe. We love to go to Raves together. The music and the crowds there almost seem like life support. The combination of the light and sound and friendship is really energizing. The drug scene is pretty intense, but I like to go sober in the crowd and afterwards do Ecstasy back at a friend's place. It's not a sex thing as much as this wonderful feeling of closeness.

I've had good sexual experiences with my friends, but I've never been in love. I'm not sure if I ever want to get married. It just seems like such a trap to have to be with this one person forever. My parents have stayed together for twenty-eight years now and I'm proud of them, but I'm not sure I could do it. Maybe the way I separate sex from love goes back to the original distrust I developed for boys after my male teenage babysitter sexually abused me when I was five years old. I thought it was my fault and I was so ashamed. Even though I had lots of therapy, it's taken me a long time to trust boys, except my dad and my brothers, who have always been totally on my side, even if they don't always tell me what I want to hear. I really love both of my parents. I know they don't always approve of my behavior, but they always love me.

I think the double standard is unfair and still around. Guys certainly don't have a problem separating sex from love, but somehow girls aren't supposed to experience desire without being "in love" first. Being at boarding school really opened my eyes to the fact that girls could be just as sexually adventurous as guys. The girls were much more likely to talk about getting laid than being in love. The important thing for me right now is that I have some really good male friends. That's a long way from not even being able to make eye contact with boys, like when I was little. Now I have three male roommates and I'm really enjoying it.

I've always questioned authority, not necessarily followed the rules, so it's not out of character for me to question an institution like marriage. I mean, I don't have pierced ears, but prefer a lip bar. I think it suits me better. It's called a labret and the definition in the dictionary is "a lip ornament worn by savage people." I like that. I don't necessarily like peoples' negative reactions to something non-traditional. When I tried to get my old job back, the manager said, "No, because your piercing is offensive." Well, I think his judgmental attitude is offensive. The funny thing is a lot of the grown-ups who disapprove of body piercing or baggy clothes probably felt misunderstood as hippies when they were young.

Richard Stiles

age 17

"When I'm with my girlfriend, it just makes me feel better about myself. I can talk to her about anything. I can cry in front of her and not feel embarrassed. Our physical closeness makes all conversation possible."

I'm starting my senior year this September and I'm excited to see my high school career coming to an end. It seems to me that most of the administration there is on a power trip, throwing their weight around just because they can. "No pass, back to class" is the motto in the nurses' station. You have to get a teacher's permission to go to the bathroom. I don't have a sense that the adults at school, like the cops on the street, are there to help you as much as bust you for doing something wrong. As a teenager, you're basically deprived of fundamental human rights. We might be younger, but we're still human. I always say, "If disrespect is presented, than present disrespect." That's why so many kids today don't respect their elders. They're just giving back what they're given. If they always treat us like we're guilty until proven innocent, then we're not going to be on their side.

It sucks that I can't walk through my own neighborhood without having to watch my back. Violence is around every corner these days and it doesn't help kids to treat all of them like they are criminals. Sometimes as a teenager, you feel really isolated and alone, like no one's on your side. My circle of friends won't back down. We won't put up with much, because it's the only way to get respect. We have a cocky attitude because of our friends standing next to us. There's power in standing united.

I guess I'd have to say that one of the best things in my life is the fact that my parents are happily married. They've been together twenty-six years and that's something to be proud of. My dad is like the metal beam that holds up the whole house. If he wasn't there, the whole thing would collapse. He's the authority in the family, and just like with the teachers at school, I sometimes have a problem with that. I hate it when he tells me what I'm thinking and he's not even close. Then there's my mom, so sweet and loving. I think I listen to her and hear what she has to say because she really listens to me. To me, her influence is just as great as my dad's, even if she doesn't come across as this authority figure.

I think their marriage has influenced my own relationship with girls. I'm not the type of guy to go from one girl to the next. I didn't loose my virginity until this summer, and it was with someone I really love and respect. We just hit it off the first time we met. It just seemed like it was something special and important. I would get a thrill, just looking at her. I couldn't believe someone so beautiful was with me. She calls me every night before I go to bed and comes to my house every morning and wakes me up. I know she's my girlfriend, but she's so pretty, I know that there's plenty of other guys who'd like to be with her too and I get jealous sometimes. Guys will holler at her, even when we're walking together holding hands and it makes me so mad. I'm a guy and I know what guys are like. I think women are great. They do three times what men do. My dad goes to work and comes home and chills in the back yard. Maybe he plants his tomato plants or mows the grass. But when my mom gets home from work, she does the laundry, cleans the house, does the grocery shopping, looks after the kids, day in and day out. She grew us inside of her body and gave birth to us. It's not fair that so many men go around thinking they are superior. That's ridiculous. Talk about unfair!

I love women. Their small bodies and soft skin are one of the most wonderful things on this earth. When I'm with my girlfriend, it just makes me feel better about myself. Loving and protecting your woman is the one thing that does make sense. I can talk to her about anything. I can cry in front of her and not feel embarrassed. Our physical closeness makes all conversation possible. Most of my friends would feel really uncomfortable if I got all emotional around them.

That's one thing that makes me sad for my generation. They have developed this attitude that they don't care about anything, even their family or girlfriends. I do. It seems like kids my age need a common cause, something that can bring them all together. It seems like there's a lot less unity in my generation than in my parents' generation. I envy the unity of the black kids at my school. There's this sense that their race makes them brothers and sisters. That's probably why there are so many white kids copying black styles in dress and language.

The drug laws in this country are really whacked and out of touch with reality. There's nothing evil about drugs. In fact, some are good. Smoking a little pot or drinking a few beers can help you relax, and what's wrong with that? It's hard to have respect for laws that don't make much sense. Look at the twenty-one-year-old legal drinking age. You mean I can go to war or get married, but I can't buy a beer? That's just ridiculous. Just like so many of the silly rules at school. Students can't order pizza at lunch and teachers can. If someone comes up to me in the halls and shoves me, I can't push them back. I can't accept "just because." That's totally unfair. My world is being disrespected by adults. My world is trying to keep from being beat up. My world is worrying about how I'm going to go to college when costs are skyrocketing. How can I ever afford to get a car? Even in school, there's so much more to learn now than when our parents were in school. It almost seems overwhelming to try to figure out how you're going to make your life work.

When you're a male teenager, people always keep their eye on you, like you're up to no good. I'm not going into a store to steal things. It makes you feel angry inside. That's probably why I like the kind of music I do. Hard-driving metal sounds like how I feel within. I'll go to my room, my safe place, where I can chill and relax. I just crank up the volume and let it rip. The lyrics remind me that my soul is mine, that no one can mess with it. I just want to do the right thing, what feels right to me. I don't see why we can't leave each other in peace.

John Slough & Caroline Irons

John: "If I had a girlfriend that was as quiet as me, we'd never be able to share our thoughts. Caroline draws me out and I get to know myself at the same time I'm learning about her." Caroline: "And if I was with someone just like me, no one would stop talking long enough to listen!"

age 17 & 16

CAROLINE: The first time I saw John was the first day of physics class and I thought, "Oh, he's really cute." I told a friend that I liked him and then another friend told me that John really liked me...

JOHN:...and someone else told me that Caroline liked me. I got kinda nervous, thinking I had to do something about this situation.

CAROLINE: I dialed his number a lot and then hung up before anyone could answer. He finally called me...

JOHN:...and I was going through my own torture. It took me days to get up the nerve to call her but by that summer, everyone we knew just thought of us as a couple...

CAROLINE:...it's always John and Caroline or Caroline and John...

JOHN: It was hard for me to say, "I love you," even when I knew I did.

CAROLINE: I said it way before he did. It was so confusing when he didn't say it back right away.

JOHN: I can't remember when I first said the words "I love you," but I'm sure Caroline can!

CAROLINE: Remember when you gave me this ring? (She holds up her hand)

JOHN: On your birthday?

CAROLINE: NO! You gave this to me for Christmas...

John: OOPS!

CAROLINE: You gave me a birthday card with my Christmas present. That's why you're confused. Remember that card that said "You're impossible to shop for?"...Then on the inside it said "Happy Birthday?"

JOHN: I guess I liked the way the card looked. I should have paid more attention to what it said, I suppose. But anyway, I finally got up the nerve to say how I felt. Now we eat lunch together at school everyday and talk on the phone, if we're not actually together, after school or on weekends.

CAROLINE: I don't drive, so John takes me anywhere I need to go. We do my mom's grocery shopping for her while she's at work.

JOHN: Sometimes we spend so much time together, I worry that I don't have enough time alone.

CAROLINE: But I'm not the type of person who enjoys being alone just to be alone...

JOHN:...That's why Caroline is so good for me. If I had a girlfriend that was as quiet as me, we'd never be able to share our thoughts. Caroline draws me out and I get to know myself at the same time I'm learning about her.

CAROLINE: And if I was with someone just like me, no one would stop talking long enough to listen! It seems like our feelings have more value over time. Even after just dating for two years, we've had our hard times, and every time we work things out, we come out on the other side a little stronger, a little closer. It's nice.

JOHN: Closeness comes from shared experience and mutual respect and that's how you learn to trust each other. It's no longer hard for me to tell Caroline that I love her.

Kelle Kasper

age 18

"One of the big problems for teenagers in my little town is there is really nothing to do and really nowhere to go. Everybody gets bored and then they end up doing something stupid and getting in trouble."

I got a baton from Santa Claus when I was five years old and I just picked it up right away. I started taking lessons and marching in parades. When I went to high school, I joined the JV and then the Varsity majorette squad. My junior and senior year, I was squad captain. We performed at football games and traveled with the school band to parades in different parts of the country, which is fine with me because I probably wouldn't get to see many other places any other way. I have so many trophies in my house from the timed competitions. We had to do a strut routine, a one-and two-baton routine, as well as model our outfits. I'm really glad I've got my baton because I've really enjoyed the whole experience. I was really shy when I was little, just always clinging to my mama's leg and someone suggested that she put me in a beauty pageant, that might help. My twirling gave me confidence in the talent part of the program and, after a while, instead of being all nervous and scared, I started really enjoying the contests.

I've lived in the same little town all my life. It's kinda good and it's kinda bad. You can't go anywhere where everybody doesn't know you, which makes you feel safe; but the bad part is since everyone knows everyone else's business, it makes for a lot of gossip, and reputations get ruined by half-truths and out-and-out untruths. Tonight at the fair, when I was crowned Queen, it was really great looking out in the audience and knowing just about everyone there. I felt like everybody was rooting for me. My boyfriend was so proud and so was my mom. She was crying, she was so happy. I've worked at Ace Hardware after school for the past two years, so there's very few people that I don't know. When I turned sixteen, my dad gave me a Mustang and everyone sure wanted to be my friend then! Some people were jealous, but people here always talk for lack of anything better to do.

One of the big problems for teenagers in my little town is there is really nothing to do and really nowhere to go. Everybody gets bored and then they end up doing something stupid and getting in trouble. Racing each other, squealing tires, vandalizing and removing signs, picking fights — all of these things are really dumb and probably not that much fun, but it's what happens for lack of anything else. Even just going out on a date can be pretty expensive, what with the prices of a movie and a restaurant meal. The guy is expected to pick up the check, so that can cost him quite a lot. I don't think the kids here are worse than anywhere else, there's just not enough to do, so they just start picking.

I basically get along with my mom as good as the next kid, not that we don't butt heads sometimes. Parents have so much power over their kids, things can never feel equal and sometimes that causes problems. She always wants me to do housework on Sunday and there's lots of other things I'd rather be doing. I usually leave right from work to go out with my boyfriend, so I don't get to see my mom and she complains about that. It seems perfectly natural to me that I would want to spend time with my friends more than with my mom at this stage of my life, but I guess it kinda hurts her feelings.

It sometimes scares me to think about having kids myself one day. I see these kids in eighth grade dressing and acting like they're all grown, when they're still just kids. A lot of kids in fifth and sixth grade are no longer innocent. It seems to me that all the drug education programs and what-not just gives them more information than they really need to have at that age. And yet when you have sex education, at least at my school, no one mentions birth control. It seems like the way our society raises kids is a little messed up. On the one hand we tell them too much, and on the other we tell them too little.

Southampton County

Timmy Piercy

age 19

> "I don't think my generation is any more crazed, or off the track than my older brothers and sister or my parents, but I think society's attitude towards teenagers has changed. Now there's much more law enforcement and mandatory sentencing. Society has a lot less tolerance for joyous excess."

I do not get embarrassed easily. That's probably why I've never hesitated to take a dare or perform a party trick. I'm not particularly worried about looking foolish. It's kinda liberating, actually. Since I'm not modest, it's easy to accept a dare to walk around naked at a party. It livens things up considerably. I'm always up for a good time, but I'm not reckless. I mean, if I take a sixty-five foot jump into the quarry, I swim around and check out the bottom first.

I'm the youngest of four, by quite a few years, and my brothers were big partyers. I can be a lot more open with Mom and Dad because they've already raised three kids, so there's not a whole lot I have to protect them from. They're definitely more easy going with me than they were with my siblings. Experience gives you some perspective on what's important. When I did mess up pretty bad, Dad had no problem punishing me and sometimes I hated him for it. But I've got to admit that his discipline taught me to accept the consequences for my behavior. At the time, I thought he was evil — I sure didn't thank him for it! Now, I realize he didn't enjoy ruining my day. That I brought things down on myself. Even though kids need to be disciplined, the flip side is if parents are too strict in high school, the kids tend to go more wild in college. There needs to be a transition between being totally sheltered and the complete freedom of not answering to anyone but yourself. It's not fair to the kid. Let him start making his own decisions while he's still living at home, before he's out in the world, unsupervised. I learned to drink responsibly the hard way, without any parental supervision. I threw up, got hung over, got into fights and ran into walls until I figured out that I didn't want that to be my way of life. A lot of the hearty partying is a guy thing. It's like we want to act like fools and then brag about it. You rarely see a girl doing an inverted keg hit. When girls do wild stuff, they certainly don't go around talking about it. Drinking games like quarters can be a lot of fun. I mean, conversation is good, but sometimes you just need to get silly.

Frankly, I don't think my generation is any more crazed, or off the track than my older brothers and sister or my parents, but I think society's attitude towards teenagers has changed. There's more DUIs today than ten or twenty years ago because the police are checking for it much more often. Marijuana possession used to be a misdemeanor, if it was even prosecuted at all. Now there's much more law enforcement and mandatory sentencing. Society has a lot less tolerance for joyous excess. Today, they'd just as soon throw you in jail and throw away the key as look at you. I have this theory that our parents' generation was pretty wild and they remember how they behaved when they were our age, so they want to lay down the law and tighten restrictions, in an attempt to control their kids' behavior. It takes a lot of courage to let your kids make their own mistakes, but that's the only way they can really learn and grow up.

Shura Baryshnikov

age 16

"The sixties was a very different time. There was a sense of community and unity in my mom's generation that we just don't have. The Vietnam War was a wake-up call that really unified a whole group of young people. Unfortunately, or maybe fortunately, we haven't woken up."

A lot of the kids that are raised in the movie industry can get pretty distorted values about money and fame. Even though I've had this unusual childhood, traveling to my mom's different movie locations all over the world, she pretty much has the same set of rules and expectations for us kids, no matter where we are. I have a summer job. I don't have a car. My parents expect for me to deserve and earn everything I get. I like wearing thrift store clothes. They're more comfortable and much more my style than some color coordinated outfit. I never have any more money in my pocket than any of my other friends in public high school.

Sometimes people expect me to have a huge stereo or TV in my room, but I don't, and I don't miss them either. When friends first come over to my house, they expect my mom to be lounging around in fancy clothes, with servants waiting on us hand and foot. They're like, "You do the dishes and clean your own room?" Mom and I both feel that if you just sit back and pay all these people to live your life for you, it's really bad karma. Wanting stuff is just a weight to get rid of.

When I was younger, instead of appreciating all the different parts of the world we'd get to see, I just wanted to stay home, go to school with my friends and play sports. I think most young teens don't appreciate change. Probably because their own bodies are changing so much, they just want to keep the rest of their world on a routine. As I'm maturing, I realize more and more how fortunate I've been. I spent part of the winter in London and this summer I got to go with my dad on tour through Greece and Turkey. Last summer we were in Bordeaux and I got to visit my dad in the Carribean. We studied Ancient Greek civilization this year in school, then I got to actually stand on the track in Olympia where the first Olympic races were run. They really had it together back then. Their motto was "Glory to the winner, honor to the loser."

I'm entering a phase in my life when I'm really interested in the spiritual nature of things. The absolutes of Christianity just seem like an intellectual exercise to me. I feel like most things in life are neither completely good nor completely evil. It's hard not to be judgmental if you think you know all the answers, and empathy and compassion are the traits I strive most to achieve. Putting compassion into action is my constant prayer.

I wear a Buddhist prayer ring with six Tibetan letters on it. They stand for Divine, Man, Earth, Water, Plant and Animal. There's a clasp on the bottom of the ring that's the sign for compassionate action and so if you are compassionate to all those six things, that creates a prayer for universal peace and that's a prayer the Tibetans have on all of their prayer wheels. When I meet someone and reach out my right hand in greeting, it's a reminder to be compassionate. We should be compassionate not only with each other, but also with ourselves. Life is a process and we should accept our actions as part of our personal history instead of having regrets. The more you respect yourself, the more you can respect others. There have been times when I'm really down on myself, and that makes it hard to feel close to other people. This summer I've grown much more comfortable and accepting of myself. I can go out of the house without wearing make up or curling my hair and still feel good about myself. I'm no longer a high-maintenance girl and I'm much more accepting of myself and others.

I remember the trauma I used to go through on the first day of the school year. I'd try on tons of different clothes and do my hair a bunch of different ways, all the time feeling anxious and insecure. At the Lillith Fair concert this summer there were so many young women there who were completely natural and completely beautiful in their attitudes towards themselves and each other and I found that really inspirational. We spun around in our long skirts all night and celebrated our female energy in the most wonderfully positive way. The strength I find with my girlfriends is incredible.

I think all kids wonder where their talent lies and here I am with my mom, who's this incredible actress, my stepfather who's this amazing writer, and my dad who's this spectacular dancer, and what's left for me but... visual art, there you go! I don't want to be like Jakob Dylan, following in his father's footsteps as a song writer. I mean, for heaven's sake! That might be great for him, but I'm not going to put myself through that hell. When I was in London last winter, I was away from all of my friends and it was a real time of introspection for me. I'd take long walks and think about who I am and where I'm going. I find tremendous satisfaction in painting and photography, but I'm a true Pisces, with lots of different enthusiasm. I love astrology and homeopathy, but I'm not sure how all these things connect, or even if they do.

My mom says she never used to worry about what she was going to be when she grew up, but the sixties was a very different time. There was a sense of community and unity in her generation that we just don't have. The Vietnam War was this event that really unified a whole group of young people, even as it separated the younger generation from their parents. My age group is totally fragmented. There's the issues of race and gender, that are really divisive. There's the punks, the preps, the stoners, the straight edgers, the Goths, and neo-hippies. We're split in a million different agendas and the result is everyone feels more insecure about the future. My friends can't just pick up and hitchhike to California — the world just doesn't seem like such a unified and friendly place for my generation. There's not that community of people that will look out for each other like there was in the sixties.

At Lillith Fair, for a few hours, we had a taste of that feeling of unity, like my mom's generation had when she was my age. Concerts are the only place where my generation can come together and have that sense of unity that sharing the music gives us. Most kids my age don't have a clue about politics. I sit in my history class and realize most of the students don't even know what a Democrat or Republican is, or have a clue about the very real horribleness of war. Vietnam was a wake-up call for my parent's generation. Unfortunately, or maybe fortunately, we haven't woken up. It seems like a lot of us are out there for ourselves more than being there for the community.

Jamez Lynch

age 17

"Where is the Martin Luther King or the Malcolm X of today? There's no public person — black or white — that kids today really admire, except the sports heroes."

I play football in the fall, basketball in the winter, and soccer and track in the spring. It seems natural for me to do four varsity sports a year because I've been involved in team sports since before I was in school. I love the mental process both before and during the game as much as the physical challenge of the sport. While my teammates whoop and holler and get themselves all pumped up to play, I find myself getting quieter and quieter, going deep inside myself to find my concentration. The most important thing my coaches have taught me is that talent isn't as important as dedication. If you show up and work hard, good things will happen to you.

My grandma is probably my biggest fan both on and off the court. She took care of me when my mom was at school and at work and got me playing soccer when I was four. She's a teacher, so I've always had a lot of respect for grades. She always said if you do good in your books, you'll do the same in sports. The dedication and concentration is the same in the classroom and on the playing field. I made the honor roll this year and that means as much to me as the points I've scored in basketball. I don't want to be bagging groceries or pumping gas for the rest of my life. I want to go to college and get a good job — one that can support a family and that I'll enjoy. Sports are a ticket for me to get into college. I mean, I love playing to win, but it's more than a game. It can help me make a future for myself. Some kids think it's cool to be hard, walking around the school pimping and everything, skipping class and hanging out. One day those guys will be working for the kids that were going to school and playing sports. Who's cool then?

My high school is definitely run by different cliques. The separations aren't so much by racial lines as by different groups and organizations. I usually sit with my teammates in the cafeteria. You sit next to your friends in the classroom and it often turns out that all the black kids are on one side of the room and all the white kids are on the other side of the room. Kids are always afraid of being accused of trying to "act black" or "act white" and that's a real shame. It really makes me mad when black kids accuse me of "acting white" because I want to make good grades. Can't a black person be smart? It seems like black culture respects sports achievements most of all. At least in my generation, more kids admire Michael Jordan than Thurgood Marshall. Back when my parents were my age, it seems like there were more impressive black leaders. Where is the Martin Luther King or the Malcolm X of today? There's no public person — black or white — that kids today really admire except the sports heroes.

When my friends and I walk down the street, you can tell it makes people nervous. Every time you see a young black male in the news or on TV, they're usually committing a crime. If you go to school and hold down a weekend job like I do, you don't hear much about it. The news tells all about the twenty black guys that jumped some poor white guy because he was trying to go to a store in their neighborhood. I guess kids like me are just not news, but that doesn't mean we don't exist, that we're less "real" than a gangsta. The headline is some kid shooting another kid and the girl that gets a perfect score on her SATs gets a little tiny mention in the back of the paper.

I hope to get a scholarship to an out-of-state school, because I'd like to experience other places. It's a big world out there and I'd like to check it out. My family, teachers, coaches and minister have taught me a lot over the years and someday soon I'd like to try the world on my own. I guess college is a good first step.

AIR
AIR

Peach Friedman

age 17

"Hearing the music is only half of it. Being part of the community in the audience is just as important. Being there is, for me, a spiritual experience. When you go to a show, the dancing is like a form of prayer."

In fourth or fifth grade I started to notice music. It's a little embarrassing now, but the first group that really "spoke" to me was New Kids on the Block. I even got a crush on Joe, the youngest member of the group. Their youth was a huge part of the attraction, I'm sure. It was like finding a spokesman for your age group. When I actually hit puberty, my musical tastes changed along with my body. I started listening to groups like Pearl Jam and Guns N' Roses — the whole angry, loud music scene. When you're an adolescent, everything's new, everything's changing within you, and you're lost somewhere between being a child and an adult. You don't understand where your place is anymore, and neither do your parents. The world seems a lot more competitive and there's this huge amount of feelings — probably unfamiliar hormones — that are confusing, and that can make you angry. There's a lot of pain because of the changes and I think for just about everyone, change is hard. As you grow taller and your body changes from a girl into a woman, it's scary because it's so out of your control — there's nothing you can do about it. I mean, you can't decide whether to get your period or not, and you can feel overwhelmed. When you're fourteen years old and some band is singing about anger and pain, you really relate to the feelings.

After a few years of adolescence, I grew out of my own angst as I got used to the changes going on in my own body and my taste in music changed to reflect my feelings. The Grateful Dead and Phish are about joy instead of anger. I feel like I've grown into myself in the last few years and I can look at kids a bit younger than me and see them in the same phase of anger and confusion that I experienced, which at the time seems like it'll last forever. The first time I saw Phish in concert, I said, "This is going to change my life." When I heard their music and shared the experience with a like-minded crowd, I felt at home for the first time in so long — like I could be totally me, surrounded by so much love. I felt so welcomed. For a band like Phish, hearing the music is only half of it, being part of the community in the audience is just as important.

Being there is, for me, a spiritual experience. I've never really believed in God in any organized religion, but I believe in the music. It's the same kind of thing as going to church. There are leaders preaching to you and you pray and you work to heal yourself and you are surrounded by people who are doing the same thing. When you go to a show, the dancing is like a form of prayer. The musicians are up there on stage, showing you the way. For me, dancing is a release. Music evokes feeling and dancing is an expression of that feeling. The experience is totally real, almost impossible to describe in words. It's really powerful, in fact, you can take it too far. At my second Phish concert I got so swept up in being part of that community, and a big part of that culture is drugs. I got so high, I ended up in the hospital. I danced so long and so hard and the crush of people around me was so intense, that I passed out cold for quite some time. I really thought I was going to die. I even hallucinated that there were two doctors hovering over me, saying I wasn't going to make it. It's hard for me to talk about the experience because it was far too intense to be understood in words. I learned a valuable lesson, though, because I no longer smoke pot and I learned I don't have to get high to enjoy a concert. In fact, it feels even better now, to go to a show and to feel like an individual instead of just part of the crowd. I really needed to learn the lesson that you don't have to get high to be high. You can love Phish like a freak without doing LSD.

My group of friends respects themselves and others, and can be more responsible than adults give us credit for. My boyfriend uses condoms. I buckle my seat belt and we have a sense of our own mortality. Like adults, we make mistakes, but by the late teens you start to have a pretty good sense of your own values.

Linnea Englblom

age 16

"I love to improvise. The feeling of actually creating original music is wonderful. Where does the music come from? I could never play so freely without all the years of practice. Hopefully all my years of religious training will one day enable me to have my faith pour out of me like notes from the strings of my violin."

It's been a struggle growing up in a devout Christian household. It's always been expected of me to follow in the exact same path of my parents and my brothers and sister. Even though I've gone to church almost every Sunday, I've always had my doubts. I could hear the minister's words and understand what he was saying, but I didn't always apply those principles to my day-to-day life. It's like I didn't want to give up the opportunity to experience different things and have fun. Yet, I'm not really sure if that kind of freedom is really freedom at all. I'm still on a journey to commit myself to God's will, as opposed to just following my immediate needs. I still don't have a personal relationship with God. Something's holding me back. I absolutely believe in the Bible, so I can't explain what is holding me back. Perhaps it's because I feel a big desire to learn about other religions. Right now I'm reading about the Hindu religion. I want to know what's out there so my decision will be based on knowledge instead of what I've always been taught since I was a child. I feel like I still have some learning to do before I can accept things finally.

I've always had a really amazing relationship with my father. Much of our discussions center around my struggle to turn over my life to God. I can talk to him about any idea that is forming in my head and just talking about it makes things seem clearer. We live in a culture that really promotes self-fulfillment, and that's at odds with the ten commandments, which demand absolute obedience to God's Law. Popular culture is interested in the short term gratification of the self, but religion teaches us that we often have to put off our immediate wants for a higher need. There's nothing much sadder than the expression "I don't care." I see my life as a gift and I don't want to waste the opportunity to contribute. You see so much ingratitude in our culture, which is pretty ironic because we have so much more than most of the world.

Of course, it's pretty impossible for anyone to never succumb to their immediate wants, especially a young person who hasn't suffered any consequences. When I was fourteen, we snuck cigarettes and beer into Bible camp. One of the most mortifying moments of my life was when my parents had to come pick me up at midnight, after I was kicked out. My parents sent me over to Sweden, to get away from negative influences, but those things are everywhere. You can't deal with it by escaping. Being there did break the cycle of just always obsessing on my social life. I learned to speak the language and got much more seriously involved with my music, so that by the time I came back home, I had a lot more self-confidence in what I could accomplish. I came back a much stronger and centered person, so I wasn't such a follower anymore. My priorities took a big shift. I wasn't so easily impressed by superficial things. Once I got to know myself better, I was able to make deeper and more meaningful relationships with others.

For years I felt like I was following in my sister's footsteps, playing the violin. I've always loved playing it, but I always struggled against practice. For a long time I was unwilling or unable to put in the hard work it takes to be really good. I love to improvise. The feeling of actually creating original music is wonderful. It's impossible for me to describe in words. I'm in awe, really. Where does the music come from? It's really incredible to play with other musicians and just play off each other, improvising back and forth. I could never play so freely without all the years of practice. Hopefully all the years of religious training that I've had will one day enable me to have my faith pour out of me like notes from the strings of my violin.

LINCOLN CENTER THEATER

Alejandra Ospina

age 17

"So far, my teenage years have been pretty defined by both physical and parental restrictions, so the theater group has been a way for me to transcend those constraints. Realizing that I could do something that not everybody could do has been really good for my confidence. I've started thinking of myself as a singer, instead of a girl who sits in a chair."

I don't know when I realized my own condition. As a young child, I think I just accepted myself as the girl who had to stay in the chair all day because I couldn't get up. When I was twelve, I started going to a summer camp for kids with disabilities. The kids found out that I could sing and encouraged me to sign up for drama. My debut on stage was a solo of "Memory," from the musical *Cats*. I had always been pretty shy, and oddly enough, performing on stage was the most fun I'd ever had. Maybe that's what it took to overcome my extreme shyness. Realizing that I could do something that not everybody could do was really good for my confidence. I started thinking of myself as a singer instead of a girl who sits in a chair.

While I was at the Louis Armstrong Middle School in Queens, there was a support group for kids with disabilities, a place where we could discuss our frustrations. It's no fun to just sit around and complain all the time, so we decided to write a play about the issues we deal with everyday. A director from Lincoln Center helped us construct *Scenes From Our Lives*. After we performed at the school, we put on the play at other places and decided to form a theater group and create new work.

Soon afterwards I auditioned for a placement in the School for Performing Arts. I sang "Climb Every Mountain" from *The Sound of Music*. I still find it unbelievable that I'm now a student there, even though I'm starting my fourth year. It's funny, but a lot of people assume I'm an art major at school, because they can't imagine a person in a wheelchair actually performing. Assumptions are on both sides of the fence. Some disabled people absolutely resent people giving them extra help, while others feel entitled, so it makes those around them uneasy because they're not sure how much assistance, if any, to offer. My wheelchair is set up without back handlebars, so it's difficult for anyone to push me, but on some inclines I could use the extra help, so people both in and out of the chair have to keep a flexible attitude. One of the issues our theater group, The Fearless Theater Company, touches on is the difference between being considerate and being patronizing. Right now we're working on a public service announcement about three guys at a party, wondering if the girl in the wheelchair would like to dance. The point is, she has individual human emotions just like everyone else and we shouldn't make assumptions about anyone.

Going to college is going to be a shock, because I'm not used to having total freedom, to come and go when I want. Sometimes I feel like I'm still waiting for my life to begin. So far my teenage years have been pretty defined by both physical and parental restrictions, so the theater group has been a way for me to transcend those constraints. Right now we're working with Children's Television Workshops to produce some skits and we're planning on filming our Lincoln Theater play, *Satchmo's Gang*, later on this year, where I sing "What A Wonderful World." I think of The Fearless Theater Company as a door that disabled kids can walk through and discover their potential on the other side.

Lydia Ooghe

age 17

"Reaching adolescence has really affected my acting career. I got too tall to play young children, and I'm too young to play women. At this point, I'm not as actively pursuing roles because I'm physically not the type to get teenage roles. I just don't look like the stereotypical highschool cheerleader, but that's O.K. because I know that my age will eventually catch up with my looks."

When I was really little, I loved to play acting games. I loved dressing up and pretending like I was another person, in another time. Acting is still for me today a joyful process of make-believe. Role playing is, oddly enough, at least for me, a process of self-discovery. My first break into professional theater came when there was an open call for young Cosette in *Les Miserables* in Washington, D.C. I was only ten years old and small for my age. When the four month run there was over, I really missed working at that level of intensity and excitement. I got an agent and a few months later I did *Les Mis* on Broadway for nine months. I left *Les Mis* after winning the role of Mary Lennox in *The Secret Garden* on Broadway. After nine months, the show closed and I joined the International Touring Company of *The Secret Garden,* which lasted another fourteen months. I came back home the week I turned fourteen.

Reaching adolescence has really affected my career. I got too mature to play children, but I'm still too young to play adults. They usually cast women eighteen and up to do teenage roles. I felt really awkward in early puberty. My nose was much bigger than the rest of my face and my feet were enormous, compared to the rest of me. At this point, I'm not as actively pursuing roles because I'm physically not the type to play teenagers. I'm not tall and blond, with regular little facial features, but I believe there will be good parts for me again when I get older. I just don't look like the stereotypical high school cheerleader, but that's O.K. because I know that my age will eventually catch up with the way I look. I'm enjoying my time off now, to make mistakes and be a kid.

Most kids want the same thing, which is acceptance and approval, whether it's through getting good grades or smoking pot. It's a conflict for kids to win acceptance from both their parents and their peers. The pressure for most teens is to win their peers' approval, because deep down they know that their parents will love them no matter what. They don't feel that other kids their age will be as accepting. Your parents are stuck with you, but your friends aren't. Another conflict is keeping your individuality while trying to fit in. When I go to an audition, I have to present myself in a strong manner, so the casting director won't forget me, but when I'm back at school, I have to tone it down, or my friends will think I'm really affected.

It used to be important to get straight As on my grades, probably because I associated it with getting good reviews. But I've relaxed a lot in the past couple of years, and grades in themselves aren't as valuable to me anymore. I'm enjoying both my social life and my class work more than I used to. It's good to have this time to think about what I want to do with my career in the future. If I were working professionally now, I wouldn't have the luxury to plan ahead. I place a lot of value on education. After college, I hope to return to New York to act.

I'm so grateful for the support my parents have given me in pursuing my acting career. My mom moved with me to New York City when I was acting, while my dad kept his medical practice going and stayed with my older brother here at home. I couldn't have accomplished what I did without their help. My mom and I built up a really good relationship when we lived in New York and toured together. We have basically the same values. I think a lot of parents just see what they want to see when it comes to their kids. They like to think their child is a perfect angel, and are careful not to ask the wrong questions.

Another type of parent always assumes their child is guilty until proven innocent. Eventually, that kid starts thinking, "I might as well enjoy all the things they already think I'm doing anyway." Fortunately for me, my parents don't fall into either category. They've found the balance between blind trust and constant suspicion.

It seems like a lot of adults get uneasy whenever there's a group of teenagers hanging around. On one hand they think, "'Oh, the poor things, they don't have anywhere else to go," and at the same time thinking, "Hmmm...No good can come of this." I think it's definitely worse for a group of boys, but of course, I can only guess. It's really weird, but I've noticed that when girls get around adults, their whole demeanor changes. Their voices rise up a few octaves and they become super friendly. I even catch myself slipping into the too-polite mode. I think we do it when we feel that adults don't trust us. It's terrible, but some adults make us feel guilty simply for existing in front of them. They've probably been influenced by the media to equate teenager with bad. All you ever hear about on the news or in the papers is teens' relationship to drugs, sex, and violence. You'd think that kids were singlehandedly responsible for all the problems in this country. We're probably only responsible for half of them. I guess blame is easier for some people than understanding.

The decade between ten and twenty is a tumultuous time. You're trying to figure out where you stand

on every issue. Even food becomes an issue. If I eat a bag of crackers, some of my friends think I'm eating too much junk food. With others, I might feel guilty if I don't join them in a bloomin' onion and a huge chocolate milkshake, because I want to stay away from the sugar and fat.

You analyze everything, even types of food. There's masculine food and feminine food. Boys usually order cheeseburgers or steak, and girls order pasta or a green salad. I think I've learned a lot about people by observing what they eat and how they eat it. Some girls are practically afraid of food, whether it's fear of getting fat or fear of being unfeminine. I used to be uncomfortable eating in front of a guy if I had a crush on him because I was afraid of getting tomato sauce on my face or spinach in my teeth. Now I'm much more relaxed at the table because I'm more relaxed with myself.

Girls and boys aren't as different as they might seem, though. Stereotypically, girls are better at describing their personal feelings, and guys don't know where to start. But most of my guy friends express themselves better than I can. Maybe they're unusual, or maybe times are changing. If anything strikes me as special about teenagers today, it's that boys and girls are less separated from each other. In the past people would date in couples on the weekends, but now we just hang out in big groups without that pressure. Guys and girls make good friends for each other because they have differences and can teach each other.

Stephanie Taylor

age 18

"For as long as I can remember, life has basically been material for my fiction. When I wrote 'Sugar Days,' I just tapped back into that hellish age of thirteen. I don't think I've ever talked to anyone who's had a happy middle school experience. You feel so self-conscious about your very existence."

I've been writing stories since before I could read or write. We still have these pages I would write when I was three years old. They're filled with crazy shapes that I can't decipher, but I'd explain to my mom that they were stories that I'd written and I'd tell her all about it and she'd write them down in legible English. My dad's a writer, so it was a natural for me to want to write books too. I'm an only child, much to my constant chagrin and dismay. You get almost an overload of parental attention, because you don't have any siblings to distract your parents. I think I put a lot of pressure on myself, knowing I'm their one shot at turning out a child that they can be proud of.

For as long as I can remember, life has basically been material for my fiction. It's a little scary, the extent to which I regard everything in the world as material for my writing. I can't stop looking at things as a writer, even when I sometimes want to. A good friend of mine committed suicide on Passover, and my very first thought when I heard about it was that I would write a poem, that it almost demanded to be a poem. I was revolted by my reaction, that I wasn't able to respond with more emotion, that I was analyzing for my writing. I think the first moment I had the absolute realization that "O.K., I'm thinking like a writer," was four years ago in France with my god-sister. We were climbing a hill to these Druid sacrificial grounds. I was just absorbed in observing the trees and the sounds, trying to imagine how it must have been for the Druids when they were walking these paths and she breaks the silence by saying, "You're making up a story about this, aren't you?" She was right. She caught me.

When I wrote "Sugar Days," I just tapped back into that hellish age of thirteen. I don't think I've ever talked to anyone who's had a happy middle school experience. You feel so self-conscious about your very existence. You're trying to find your own identity at the same time you're under tremendous pressure to conform with your peers. The confusion gave me a lot of anger. I think that's one reason seventh and eighth grade girls are so mean to each other — everyone's confused and angry. Back then, everything is so dramatic and elevated in importance. In my short story, I identify with the girl who is fearful to eat. Food is such an issue for teenage girls, because we're terrified of getting fat and place great value on thinness. Anorexia is partly a way of trying to gain control, when your life feels so out of control. In my story, the girl who won't eat is trying to relieve some of the weight of her guilt by losing her physical weight.

In your early teens, everyone looks at each other with such scrutiny, everyone feels either too fat or too thin. There's almost nothing you can do about it when your body starts to change. For every girl I know, their body is an issue. I was super skinny in early puberty and people would always ask me if I was anorexic. I was just naturally thin, but I felt really apologetic about it. I think some girls use anorexia not only to try to control their changing bodies, but also to punish themselves, to try and combat a guilty conscience. It's about having such low self-esteem that you think you don't deserve to live.

highground

Shelia Motley

age 16

"After years of competing in horse shows, I put the same high expectations on myself in school as well. It's not good enough to do average work. I can't help trying to do my best."

Even though both of my parents are in the horse business, I never really felt any pressure to ride. It's more like the opportunity was always there. Once I started competing in horse shows on the weekends, riding became more than a hobby. It's like I found a place outside of my school and family where I really fit in. When I was younger I used to like to ride more than compete, but now I much prefer competition to just hacking around. I don't ride just to win anymore. In each event I'm usually working on improving one specific goal.

I've just moved on from Hunters to Jumpers. That's been a goal of mine for a long time. After years and years of competing in Hunter classes, I got really tired of it, but I'm glad I kept going and now I face a whole new set of challenges. It's almost like you have to ride so much to get to the next level that I suspect that everyone who advances along has times when they're restless and bored. Now everything seems exciting and new again.

After I graduate from high school next year, I think I'd like to take a year to ride professionally and see if I like it at that level. I know that the time and commitment it takes to compete at the level I'm riding now would make going to college pretty difficult. The next year with the Jumpers will tell if I'll go professional. After years of competing in horse shows, I put the same high expectations on myself in school as well. It's not good enough to do average work. It's like I turn everything into a competition. I can't help trying to do my best. If anything, I'm always struggling to try to compromise a bit. For me, competition is fun. I wish I could say I'm better at not winning, but frankly, I still hate it.

When you are a little girl, at first it's amazing that you can control such a large animal. But as you spend more and more time riding, it's almost as if the horse you're riding becomes an extension of yourself. When I walk the course before a competition, I can't believe the jumps are so big. It seems unbelievable that the horse will have the athletic ability to do it. I have tremendous respect for what they can do.

Matt Lange

age 17

"Everything on the outside looks great. I'm captain of the football team, I make good grades, and have a great family and friends, but in a strange way, it's kind of isolating. Sometimes I feel like people around me would almost like to see me stumble and fall. Of course, it's never said aloud, at least to my face, but it's just a feeling I get. I feel like I don't have the luxury to make any excuses."

My dad played football in high school and college and had an offer to play professional ball, but he had a hurt back, so he didn't want to pursue it. I went to the chiropractor myself this week. It's inevitable that you're going to get some injuries, running into people all the time. I don't even remember the first time I had a football in my hand — probably in my crib! Both of my brothers play, too. Back in the fifth and sixth grade teams, my mom used to offer me money not to play because she was so worried about me getting hurt, but she's always gone to all my games and given me a lot of support.

I'm one of the team captains this year and our goal is the state championship. At last night's game, I didn't get fed the ball too many times, which I wasn't expecting to, but my dad got a little upset about that and exchanged some words with the coach, even though I had asked him not to. But he really gets carried away with the game sometimes. For him, it's hard to be objective up there in the stands when his son is out on the field.

Football is a big deal in our school, not only for the players but pretty much the rest of the town. Our coach has been at Stillwater for forty years, so there's this tremendous crowd of faithful alumni at all the games. Probably half the players' fathers had the same coach, so as you can imagine, there's always a big turnout on Friday nights. That enthusiasm from the sidelines really gets us fired up on the field. I can remember very clearly what it felt like to see the Ponies run out on the field when I was a kid. I never missed a game — nobody did. Today, all the little kids stand by the locker room and give us high fives when we leave the field. Thank goodness we do have such a good football program, because there's not a whole lot else to do but go to the games.

The turn-out probably inspires us to stay in training during the summer when school is not in session. The weight room is open all year and we have to sign in every time we work out, so coach can make sure we're staying in shape for the three-a-day practice in August. From nine to noon, then one to two, and then three to six, we work as hard as is humanly possible. The program really consumes you, from what you eat to when you sleep. We work so hard, but how great is anything that you didn't have to work for? It's almost like the more effort you put into it, the more it's worth to you. A free ride is never as meaningful as something you've really struggled for.

The tough thing about being a captain is you're supposed to make sure your teammates show up at the gym and if they break training rules at a party, I'm supposed to notice. It's hard to slack off yourself, because everyone supposedly looks to you for leadership. When school is in session, we really don't have any free time. By the time you get your homework done, you don't have a whole lot of time to get in trouble!

We haven't lost a game during regular season since I started playing varsity, so the pressure to maintain that record is intense. All the teams we come up against are really gunning for us. No other schools like us. Everyone thinks we're conceited and cocky. To beat us is something every team we play really wants. When we lost in the semi-finals last year, after a 26-game winning streak, it was such a horrible combination of frustration and disbelief. You're left looking at the clock, in shock. Not only is the game over, but the whole season is — bam! — gone. We felt like we'd let down the entire community.

STILLWATER
4

I also have a lot of pressure on me right now to choose and get accepted at a good college. My parents have taken me all over to look at schools. My dad, of course, would like to see me get a football scholarship, but I don't know if I'm so much for that because that's not really how I see myself next year. I love the game and this year is the culmination of a lifelong dream, to lead the Ponies to a state championship. When we won the title my sophomore year, oh, what a reception we got back home! The police gave our school bus an escort through town and we were hanging out the windows, screaming and yelling to all the fans who were waiting back in the freezing cold to greet us. Later they gave us a big parade.

Realistically, I realize that being a part of this team is going to be the highlight of my football career. I'm a hardworking, enthusiastic player, but I have no delusion that I'm some sort of great talent. I'm sure I could go on and play college ball at a division II or III school, but I don't want to pass up any good educational opportunities just so I can play football. After a lifetime of Minnesota winters, I wouldn't mind going someplace warm. I've always wanted to learn how to surf, so who knows? I'm looking forward to four years when I have all the freedom of an adult, but none of the responsibility.

I've always been able to get good grades. In fact, I found myself in the same situation as in football. Just like we'd never lost a conference game since I started, I'd never made anything but straight As. Last semester, I made my first B, and, in a weird way, it was a relief. Holding that 4.0 GPA is like a weight that wants to fall. So when it actually does, it's good to know that it's not the end of the world.

I have no idea what I want to be when I grow up and I worry about it every day. My dad's a pilot and that has a lot of pluses — the good pay, the travel, the 20 days off a month — but unfortunately, the best aviation school, outside of the military, is in North Dakota. So much for my surfing fantasy if I went there! People ask so casually, "What do you want to do when you get out of school?" To me, it's not a casual question. Everything on the outside looks great. I'm captain of the football team, I make good grades and have a great family and friends, but in a strange way, it's kind of isolating. Sometimes I feel like people around me would almost like to see me stumble and fall. Of course, it's never said aloud, at least to my face, but it's just a feeling I get.

When I took my ACTs, my scores were so high, when people asked me what I got, I said I didn't get them back yet. I don't tell my friends when I get a good grade on a big paper, because they'd think I was bragging. I want to join in and complain about a test, but I'm not allowed to do that because everyone knows, including myself, that I probably did fine. I feel like I don't have the luxury to make any excuses.

Charlie Fleet

age 18

"Your first year here you're totally broken down — mentally, physically, and emotionally pushed to your limits. Then the next three years you're built back up with a set of values that will stay with you always. It's good for me, even if it is not always fun."

My dad, grandfather and great uncle all went to Virginia Military Institute. When you first get here, they scream at you, "Why did you come here? Why did you come to my school?" It's an important question that takes a while to answer. Even though I'm wearing a military uniform, I don't think of myself as a military man. My first semester, cadets would scream at me and yell at me and drop me for push-ups a million times. I soon realized that the way to survive was not to get angry, but to be non-judgmental. What happens to you during your "rat" year is so immense, it can't be described. There's nothing you can say or do that is right. You loose all concept of time because each day is exactly the same. The weeks fly by but every hour seems like an eternity. Every moment is so structured that it forces you to take pleasure in things that you used to take for granted when you had more free time. I never really appreciated a sunrise or a sunset before I got here.

Your first year here you're totally broken down — mentally, physically and emotionally pushed to your limits. Then the next three years you're built back up with a set of values that will stay with you always. The discipline gives you organizational skills that are wonderful. I haven't been late in almost a year now. You learn to never make any excuses. This place teaches you to be accountable for your behavior. If there are no excuses, you learn very quickly to prepare for the unexpected. The rank structure teaches you to be accountable not only for your own behavior, but the actions of those serving under you. Even though I have no intention of joining the military after I graduate, the accountability that I learn here can certainly be applied to any profession.

The uniforms we wear here stand for a certain code of ideals, but we're still individuals underneath, who are trained to be hardworking, efficient, and trustworthy. The system teaches us to all be the same, but that in turn forces you to appreciate your own personal experiences. When everything you enjoy is taken away from you, it makes you appreciate the things you used to take for granted. So ironically, you get to know yourself better by having your identity taken away. I believe the values and attitudes that I'm taking out of VMI are positive and worthwhile. It's good for me, even if it is not always fun.

Anne Mills

age 15

"Americans have this misguided idea that everyone's equal, which is ridiculous. If everyone is the same, things stagnate. The whole foundation of genetics is based on diversity. Life can only evolve when there's someone reaching beyond the boundaries."

I'm a big advocate of selfishness. If you do everything for your own self-interest, it tends to be good for other people. If your definition of love is self-sacrifice, then that's not really very complimentary to those you love. It's patronizing instead of respectful. Self-reliance isn't about abusing others, it's about not demanding that others are responsible for your welfare. As a female, I find affirmative action horribly insulting. I don't need any special privileges because of my sex.

Stephen Hawking, Carl Sagan and Ayn Rand are my three heroes. Americans have this misguided idea that everyone's equal, which is ridiculous. If everyone is the same, things stagnate. The whole foundation of genetics is based on diversity. Life can only evolve when there's someone reaching beyond the boundaries. I mean, certainly, Stephen Hawking contributes much more to our intellectual dialog than I do! A few years ago, I wrote a short story about a man who was completely independent, who did everything for himself. My parents read it and said it reminded them of the philosophy in *Atlas Shrugged*. I started reading it and ended up reading Rand's other novels as well. It is so exciting to discover a voice that really articulates the things you believe to be true. I've always been a voracious reader and was horribly ostracized in middle school because I enjoyed learning. At least in high school, there are more like-minded citizens. At least kids aren't afraid to think, even though I don't always agree with their thinking and you can still be ostracized for having a difference of opinion. I know some people call me "baby killer" behind my back. I told my Health class that I dreamed I had a baby and put it in a jar because I didn't want it. When the kids in class asked me if I'd really "do that" I flippantly replied, "At this age? I'd get someone else to put it in a jar for me!"

I've been dressing mostly in black recently, not because I have violent tendencies or want to kill myself, but because it expresses the seriousness of my nature. It seems like a more thoughtful form of dress, just like a frown is usually the expression you wear when you're deep in thought. In adolescence, everyone is trying to claw themselves a niche somewhere. I have always been determined not to change myself in order to fit in and belong. And even though there's a part of everyone that wants to be an individual, there's also a part of us that wants to find a group they can belong to and still feel good about themselves. I'm not much of a team player, and my friends are the same way, individuals more than joiners or leaders. I hate to have to do school projects with a partner. Recently, I had to write a paper with another student. I don't even want to try to synchronize my mind with someone else's, I'm too much of an individualist. Contrary to popular opinion, not all teenagers are bleating sheep, blindly following their peers.

Individual thought is very important to me. I don't do any drugs because I don't want to evade or deny reality, no matter how painful or difficult. You can't ultimately escape what's real, you can only get off track and lost. Mind-altering substances take you away from yourself and ultimately, that's all you have, so why throw it away? Every great thing ever done requires some degree of suffering, and I want to be as fearlessly honest as I can while I'm alive.

The trend in our culture right now is that our feelings are sacred. It's a rejection of thought and reason. Look at the popularity of horoscopes. We should follow our logic instead of our emotions. If you give up the power of your rational thought, your feelings can take over like irrational monsters, dictators. Science is my religion. Mankind invented religions to answer the questions that science now addresses.

Kristin Johnson

age 16

> "One concept that really fascinates me is post-modern thinking — the idea that there is no absolute truth, and how all history is relative. We re-write it according to how we want to see it and how we are able to see it, given our own time and place in history."

When I was in seventh grade, I had a bad case of mono and missed a whole semester of school. I had to learn the self discipline of learning on my own, because I had to be home schooled. Every now and then my mom would take me out so I could get some fresh air. I picked up a copy of *Crime and Punishment* at the German Institute, having never even heard of it. It smelled really good and was a nice size, so I bought it. When I got it home, I couldn't put it down. I absolutely loved it. I immediately jumped into more Dostoevsky, and moved on to more Russian authors, which spawned a love of literature in general. Both Dostoevsky and Tolstoy incorporate the gospel into their work, and I'm probably more interested in the philosophy or point of view of the author than the narrative of the story.

In eighth grade I got Lyme disease and had to miss another semester of school, so once again I found myself with time on my hands to do research. I was too weak to walk around much, so when I was taken on an outing to the library, I had to sit down and read, because I didn't have the energy to roam around. Puberty wasn't as traumatic for me as it is for a lot of people, because I was so isolated during seventh and eighth grade, that I escaped all the insecurity that comes from comparing yourself with others, which adolescents tend to do a lot. The school day stretches out for eight hours, but there's basically only a couple of hours of learning. The rest of the time is busywork — babysitting, really. That year I was home from school, I'd get my homework done in a short amount of time, then have the rest of the day to learn about things that really interested me. I still sometimes resent that in school it takes a whole hour to go over something that would take me five minutes at home. Yet I also realize that being in school affords me all kinds of intangible lessons in getting along in this world.

The English paper I write for my teacher is much more about trying to give her what she expects than taking any intellectual risks. Getting straight As proves that you're good at school, but it doesn't necessarily prove that you have intellectual curiosity. At sixteen, I realize I could never dazzle the teacher with my intellectual prowess anyway, so I might as well figure out what he wants me to say and how to say it. Being sick at home all that time taught me not to worry about what you're missing, because everything, basically, is an opportunity. Just learning how to negotiate the halls and find the right classrooms is an important lesson in life. No wonder so many adults still have school anxiety dreams!

This year I get to study Russian in school and it's my hope that one day I'll be able to read my favorite writers in their native language. Last summer I got to go with my dad on a business trip to Germany. It really inspired me to become fluent in a foreign language. It was wonderful to actually be in Europe. After reading so much about the culture, it seemed strangely familiar. The more I learn, the more I want to learn. I love how everything is connected and influences everything else.

One concept that really fascinates me is post-modern thinking — the idea that there is no absolute truth, and how all history is relative. When you read a book on women in the middle ages, it was written long after they existed, because no one was interested in women back then. They weren't educated to read and write, so they couldn't write about themselves. Now there are entire academic departments that focus on Medieval women. It's as if feminism has given a voice to generations of women in the past who had no voice. History changes every day. We re-write it according to how we want to see it and how we are able to see it, given our own time and place in history.

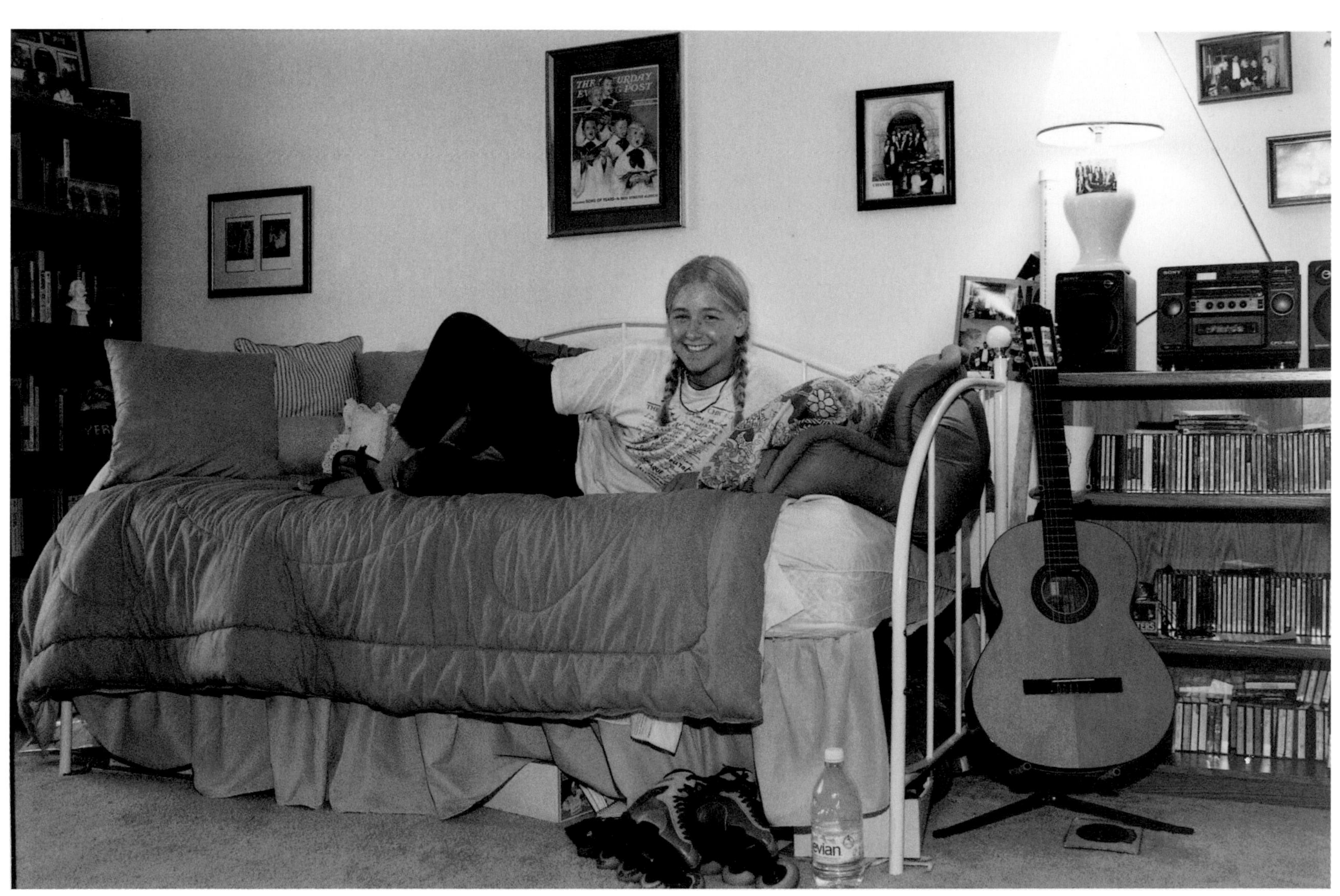
evian

Naomi, Esther & Hannah Toporovsky

Naomi: "A lot of young people are smarter than adults give them credit for." Hannah: "Kids are the future — they're full of ideas and enthusiasm." Esther: "Older people tend to say, 'It's always been this way,' and accept it, whereas young people question everything. Being negative isn't the way to effect positive change. Enthusiasm is its own type of wisdom."

age 16

ESTHER: When we were younger, we were always invited places together, but now we have more individual friendships. Because we all have different strengths and weaknesses, each of us is attracted to different people. We have our own separate best friends, even though we consider ourselves our best friends.

NAOMI: Hannah's always considered the talkative one, Esther's the logical one, and I'm really shy.

ESTHER: Naomi has the reputation as the quiet one, but it's only compared to Hannah and me that she'd be considered shy.

HANNAH: You do find your label influencing your personality. When we're together, people will always talk to me first, because I'm the talkative one. I've really become the spokesperson for the three of us — not that all of us aren't secure and strong in our own opinions. This can sometimes be pretty intimidating to guys our age. We're not desperate for a partner because we've already got each other.

NAOMI: If Hannah has an argument with her boyfriend, it's like she's got extra back-up support from Esther and me.

HANNAH: Of course, I'm always on my sisters' side. Guys don't seem to like it when girls stand up for what they believe in. It's almost like they need girls to be insecure. We're very big on equal rights and insecure guys are threatened by this. Girls that think they will find happiness through a boy's approval can easily end up with real disappointment.

ESTHER: Because our parents raised us with respect, we respect ourselves and we respect our parents. If I go out, I always let them know where I am and what I'm doing — not because they don't trust me — but because they love me.

NAOMI: Most of our friends don't have as much respect for their own parents as we do for ours. They see them as authority figures — laying down the rules and doling out the punishments. There's no trust going either way. It's sad really, because everyone is missing out on a lot.

HANNAH: Our parents raised us to speak our minds. We are just as comfortable talking to adults as we are to kids. Grown-ups are just people who are older than us.

ESTHER: Some of our friends' parents are taken aback by our outspokenness. They think people our age are just supposed to listen and obey. It's not that we don't listen, it's just that we express our opinions. What an awful idea, "Children are to be seen and not heard." Our eyes are wide open and we have a lot to say.

NAOMI: A lot of young people are smarter than adults give them credit for.

HANNAH: Kids are the future — they're full of ideas and enthusiasm.

NAOMI: Their energy makes them not afraid of change.

ESTHER: Our parents lived through the sixties. We know that change is possible. People can make a difference. Older people tend to say, "It's always been this way," and accept it whereas young people question everything. Being negative isn't the way to effect positive change. Enthusiasm is its own type of wisdom.

HANNAH: Age is just a number. Maturity is much more than that.

Acknowledgments

I send much gratitude to my book packager, Gary Chassman — I wish we'd met four books ago! Thanks for introducing me to Stacey Hood, who made designing this book a pleasure. Most of all, I acknowledge the inspirational collaboration of the kids in these pages, for without their belief in the project, there would be no book.

Thanks —

Mary